# A MARRIAGE AGREEMENT AND OTHER ESSAYS

## FOUR DECADES OF FEMINIST WRITING

# A MARRIAGE AGREEMENT AND OTHER ESSAYS

## FOUR DECADES OF FEMINIST WRITING

ALIX KATES SHULMAN

OPEN ROAD

INTEGRATED MEDIA

NEW YORK

*A Marriage Agreement* by Alix Kates Shulman

Copyright © 2012 by Alix Kates Shulman

Cover design by Andrea C. Uva

ISBN 978-1-4532-5514-8

This edition published in 2012 by
Open Road Integrated Media, Inc.
345 Hudson Street
New York, NY 10014
www.openroadmedia.com

*For Ellen Willis (1941–2006) and for Emily*

# CONTENTS

# INTRODUCTION

IT WAS IN 1967, in the midst of that decade of emotional upheaval and political dissent, that I heard the first rumblings of the women's liberation movement. News reached me in my Greenwich Village apartment via the radio, while I was washing the dinner dishes. I was in my thirties, raising two small children and beginning to write.

On the air, several fervent young women were discussing the injustice of women's situation in words that spoke directly to me. When they invited their listeners to attend an upcoming meeting of the fledgling movement, I put down my sponge and picked up my pen. Jotting down the telephone number and date of the meeting, in that moment I launched myself into one of the great liberation movements of our time, which profoundly transformed the lives of women worldwide, mine included.

Soon I joined Redstockings, one of New York's first radical feminist groups. By then the young movement had put out broadsides by individual women on a range of issues but had yet to publish a comprehensive essay about sex. I volunteered to write one. In "Organs and Orgasms" I enlisted my scholarly skills to expose male bias in current sex research. Sex is always a juicy topic, and that piece debuted in the then-infamous *Evergreen Review*, but to my surprise it was a different essay I wrote around that time, "A Marriage Agreement," proposing that men and women share all housework and childcare equally, that provoked the enormous response, both enthusiastic and dismissive. (In "A Marriage Disagreement," written years later, I revealed the secrets behind that still-controversial proposal.)

Those early essays, written when the movement was young, outrageous, and explosive, were great fun to write. So were my 1970s novels, *Memoirs of an Ex-Prom Queen*, which dramatized why a movement was needed, and *Burning Questions*, a historical novel describing the rise of the movement itself. If those pieces now leave young readers, who grew up breathing feminist ideas, feeling more advanced than me, so much the better. It means that nowadays women expect to have more orgasms and expect men to wash more dishes (though, alas, not all their expectations will be fulfilled).

By the early 1980s the explosive phase of the movement was over, at least for the time being—explosive and quiescent phases having alternated for several hundred years. Yet throughout that decade and the following, the ideas advanced by the movement were so warmly embraced by the mainstream that their very success sparked an organized, sometimes virulent backlash (including widespread bombings of abortion clinics and torture of gays), producing what became known as the culture wars.

In those politically confusing times, when our protests often felt ineffective, I was occupied writing books and teaching writing, sometimes in such alluring places as Maine, Colorado, and Hawaii. So it's no wonder that my essays focused mainly on writing. During a culture war a literary essay may be a missile.

Then, as the twentieth century segued into the twenty-first, I entered old age, as will happen to the lucky. Several events that should shock no one somehow walloped me. First, my aged parents died on my watch (inspiring my memoir *A Good Enough Daughter*). Then my friends and comrades began to die, making me a connoisseur of memorials and an author of obituaries. Finally, my 75-year-old husband fell nine feet from a sleeping loft, causing a traumatic brain injury that left him with severe dementia and led me to advocate for the elderly. (Too bad that we who once marched for free universal child care weren't prescient enough to also demand free elder care for the nearly half of those over eighty who will wind up with dementia.)

Advocates, no matter how old, face forward and upward toward the light; funerals can only momentarily divert them. This upward gaze has always marked my work, including my memoir about my husband's decline, *To Love What Is*, and the essays in the final section of this book. Whether taking stock, as in "Thoughts at Seventy," or claiming the respect due me as a Jew in "Summer Jew" or due my disabled husband in my essays about dealing with his dementia, I find myself on the eve of eighty still squinting up at the sun, despite the persistence of some of the very injustices that first made me an activist and writer.

In summer 2011, forty-two years after I wrote "A Marriage Agreement," *Time* ran a cover story called "Chore Wars" on current domestic gender imbalances. Four decades after we successfully legalized abortion and in face of a citizenry overwhelmingly in favor of contraception and abortion, several states are proposing annoying initiatives to endow fertilized eggs with the rights of persons at the expense of the rights of women. In our violent world, girls are trafficked everywhere, and recently in Afghanistan two more women accused of adultery were stoned and killed. The crazed killer who massacred scores of Norwegians in 2011 blamed his rage partly on feminist ideas, citing in his 1,500-page manifesto the writings of Betty Friedan and my brilliant Redstockings sister, the late Ellen Willis. (This called to mind the 1989 Quebec Massacre of female students by a gunman who shouted as he opened fire, "I hate feminists!") But, as I try to show in "The Kenning," the final piece in this collection, each generation can do no more than add its bit to the endless river of consciousness and change, and that's about as good as it gets.

Alix Kates Shulman
New York City

# A MARRIAGE AGREEMENT AND OTHER ESSAYS

## FOUR DECADES OF FEMINIST WRITING

# MARRIAGE AND MEN

# A MARRIAGE AGREEMENT

WHEN MY HUSBAND AND I were first married, a decade ago, keeping house was less a burden than a game. We both worked full time in New York City, so our small apartment stayed empty most of the day and taking care of it was very little trouble. Twice a month we'd spend Saturday cleaning and doing our laundry at the laundromat. We shopped for food together after work, and though I usually did the cooking, my husband was happy to help. Since our meals were simple and casual, there were few dishes to wash. We occasionally had dinner out and usually ate breakfast at a diner near our offices. We spent most of our free time doing things we enjoyed together, such as taking long walks in the evenings and spending weekends in Central Park. Our domestic life was beautifully uncomplicated.

When our son was born, our domestic life suddenly became *quite* complicated; and two years later, when our daughter was born, it became impossible. We automatically accepted the traditional sex roles that society assigns. My husband worked all day in an office; I left my job and stayed at home, taking on almost all the burdens of housekeeping and child rearing.

When I was working I had grown used to seeing people during the day, to having a life outside the home. But now I was restricted to the company of two demanding preschoolers and to the four walls of an apartment. It seemed unfair that while my husband's life had changed little when the children were born, domestic life had become the only life I had.

I tried to cope with the demands of my new situation, assuming that other women were able to handle even larger families with ease and still find time for themselves. I couldn't seem to do that.

We had to move to another apartment to accommodate our larger family, and because of the children, keeping it reasonably neat took several hours a day. I prepared half a dozen meals every day for from one to four people at a time—and everyone ate different food. Shopping for this brood—or even just running out for a quart of milk—meant putting on snowsuits, boots and mittens; getting strollers or carriages up and down the stairs; and scheduling the trip so it would not interfere with one of the children's feeding or nap or illness or some other domestic job. Laundry was now a daily chore. I seemed to be working every minute of the day—and still there were dishes in the sink: still there wasn't time enough to do everything.

Even more burdensome than the physical work of housekeeping was the relentless responsibility I had for my children. I loved them, but they seemed to be taking over my life. There was nothing I could do or even contemplate without first considering how they would be affected. As they grew older just answering their constant questions ruled out even a private mental life. I had once enjoyed reading, but now if there was a moment free, instead of reading for myself, I read to them. I wanted to work on my own writing, but there simply weren't enough hours in the day. I had no time for myself: the children were always *there*.

As my husband's job began keeping him at work later and later—and sometimes taking him out of town—I missed his help and companionship. I wished he would come home at six o'clock and spend time with the children so they could know him better. I continued to buy food with him in mind and dutifully set his place at the table. Yet sometimes whole weeks would go by without his having dinner with us. When he did get home the children often were asleep, and we both were too tired ourselves to do anything but sleep.

We accepted the demands of his work as unavoidable. Like most couples we assumed that the wife must accommodate to the husband's schedule, since it is his work that brings in the money.

As the children grew older I began free-lance editing at home. I felt I had to squeeze it into my "free" time and not allow it to interfere with my domestic duties or the time I owed my husband—just as he felt he had to squeeze in time for the children during weekends. We were both chronically dissatisfied, but we knew no solutions.

After I had been home with the children for six years I began to attend meetings of the newly formed women's liberation movement in New York City. At these meetings I began to see that my situation was not uncommon; other women too felt drained and frustrated as housewives and mothers. When we started to talk about how we would have chosen to arrange our lives, most of us agreed that even though we might have preferred something different, we had never felt we had a choice in the matter. We realized that we had slipped into full domestic responsibility simply as a matter of course, and it seemed unfair.

When I added up the chores I was responsible for they amounted to a hectic 6 A.M.–9 P.M. (often later) job, without salary, breaks or vacation. No employer would be able to demand these hours legally, but most mothers take them for granted—as I did until I became a feminist.

For years mothers like me have acquiesced to the strain of the preschool years and endless household maintenance without any real choice. Why, I asked myself, should a couple's decision to have a family mean that the woman must immerse years of her life in their children? And why should men like my husband miss caring for and knowing their children?

7

Eventually, after an arduous examination of our situation, my husband and I decided that we no longer had to accept the sex roles that had turned us into a lame family. Out of equal parts love for each other and desperation at our situation, we decided to re-examine the patterns we had been living by, and, starting again from scratch, to define our roles for ourselves.

WE BEGAN BY AGREEING TO share completely all responsibility for raising our children (by then aged five and seven) and caring for our household. If this new arrangement meant that my husband would have to change his job or that I would have to do more free-lance work or that we would have to live on a different scale, then we would. It would be worth it if it could make us once again equal, independent and loving as we had been when we were first married.

Simply agreeing verbally to share domestic duties didn't work, despite our best intentions. And when we tried to divide them "spontaneously" we ended up following the traditional pattern. Our old habits were too deep-rooted. So we sat down and drew up a formal agreement, acceptable to both of us, that clearly defined the responsibilities we each had.

It may sound a bit formal, but it has worked for us. Here it is:

**MARRIAGE AGREEMENT**

## I. Principles

We reject the notion that the work which brings in more money is more valuable. The ability to earn more money is a privilege which must not be compounded by enabling the larger earner to buy out of his/her duties and put the burden either on the partner who earns less or on another person hired from outside. We believe that each partner has an equal right to his/her own time, work, value, choices. As long as all duties are performed, each of us may use his/her extra time any way he/she chooses. If he/she wants to use it making money, fine. If he/she wants to spend it with spouse, fine. If not, fine.

As parents we believe we must share all responsibility for taking care of our children and home—not only the work but also the responsibility. At least during the first year of this agreement, *sharing responsibility* shall mean dividing the *jobs* and dividing the *time*.

In principle, jobs should be shared equally, 50-50, but deals may be made by mutual agreement. If jobs and schedule are divided on any other than a 50-50 basis, then at any time either party may call for a re-examination and redistribution of jobs or a revision of the schedule. Any deviation from 50-50 must be for the convenience of both parties. If one party works overtime in any domestic job, he/she must be compensated by equal extra work by the other. The schedule may be flexible but changes must be formally agreed upon. The terms of this agreement are rights and duties, not privileges and favors.

## II. Job Breakdown and Schedule

### (A) Children

1. Mornings: Waking children: getting their clothes out; making their lunches; seeing that they have notes, homework, money, bus passes, books; brushing their hair; giving them breakfast (making coffee for us). Every other week each parent does all.

2. Transportation: Getting children to and from lessons, doctors, dentists (including making appointments), friends' houses, park, parties, movies, libraries. Parts occurring between 3 and 6 P.M. fall to wife. She must be compensated by extra work from husband (see 10 below). Husband does all weekend transportation and pickups after 6.

3. Help: Helping with homework, personal problems, projects like cooking, making gifts, experiments, planting; answering questions, explaining things. Parts occurring between 3 and 6 P.M. fall to wife. After 6 P.M. husband does Tuesday, Thursday and Sunday: wife does Monday, Wednesday and Saturday. Friday is free for whoever has done extra work during the week.

4. Nighttime (after 6 P.M.): Getting children to take baths, brush their teeth, put away their toys and clothes, go to bed; reading with them; tucking them in and having nighttime talks; handling if they wake or call in the night. Husband does Tuesday, Thursday and Sunday. Wife does Monday, Wednesday and Saturday. Friday is split according to who has done extra work during the week.

5. Baby sitters: Getting baby sitters (which sometimes takes an hour of phoning). Baby sitters must be called by the parent the sitter is to replace. If no sitter turns up, that parent must stay home.

6. Sick care: Calling doctors; checking symptoms; getting prescriptions filled; remembering to give medicine; taking days off to stay home with sick child; providing special activities. This must still be worked out equally, since now wife seems to do it all. (The same goes for the now frequently declared school closings for so-called political protests, whereby the mayor gets credit at the expense of the mothers of young children. The mayor closes only the schools, not the places of business or the government offices.) In any case, wife must be compensated (see 10 below).

7. Weekends: All usual child care, plus special activities (beach, park, zoo). Split equally. Husband is free all Saturday, wife is free all Sunday.

## (B) Housework

8. Cooking: Breakfast; dinner (children, parents, guests). Breakfasts during the week are divided equally: husband does all weekend breakfasts (including shopping for them and dishes). Wife does all dinners except Sunday nights. Husband does Sunday dinner and any other dinners on his nights of responsibility if wife isn't home. Whoever invites guests does shopping, cooking and dishes: if both invite them, split work.

9. Shopping: Food for all meals, housewares, clothing and supplies for children. Divide by convenience. Generally, wife does local daily food shopping: husband does special shopping for supplies and children's things.

10. Cleaning: Dishes daily; apartment weekly, biweekly or monthly. Husband does dishes Tuesday, Thursday and Sunday. Wife does them Monday, Wednesday and Saturday. Friday is split according to who has done extra work during week. Husband does all the house cleaning in exchange for wife's extra child care (3 to 6 daily) and sick care.

11. Laundry: Home laundry, making beds, dry cleaning (take and pick up). Wife does home laundry. Husband does dry-cleaning delivery and pickup. Wife strips beds, husband remakes them.

OUR AGREEMENT CHANGED our lives. Surprisingly, once we had written it down we had to refer to it only two or three times. But we still had to work to keep the old habits from intruding. If it was my husband's night to take care of the children, I had to be careful not to check up on how he was managing. And if the baby sitter didn't show up for him, I would have to remember it was *his* problem.

Eventually the agreement entered our heads, and now, after two successful years of following it, we find that our new roles come to us as readily as the old ones had. I willingly help my husband clean the apartment (knowing it is his responsibility) and he often helps me with the laundry or the meals. We work together and trade off duties with ease now that the responsibilities are truly shared. We each have less work, more hours together and less resentment.

Before we made our agreement I had never been able to find the time to finish even one book. Over the past two years I've written three children's books, a biography and a novel and edited a collection of writings (all will have been published by spring of 1972). Without our agreement I would never have been able to do this.

At present my husband works a regular 40-hour week, and I write at home during the six hours the children are in school. He earns more money now than I do, so his salary covers more of our expenses than the money I make with my free-lance work. But if either of us should change jobs, working hours or income, we would probably adjust our agreement.

Perhaps the best testimonial of all to our marriage agreement is the change that has taken place in our family life. One day after it had been in effect for only four months our daughter said to my husband, "You know, Daddy, I used to love Mommy more than you, but now I love you both the same."

# A MARRIAGE DISAGREEMENT,
# OR MARRIAGE BY OTHER MEANS

EARLY IN 1969, WHEN MY children were five and seven, I wrote "A Marriage Agreement" proposing that the tasks of child care and housework be divided equally between husband and wife. Like most women of my class and generation born in the United States before World War II, I had accepted, if sometimes grudgingly, traditional gender arrangements whereby the home belongs to women, the world to men. But during the previous year, when the electrifying ideas of women's liberation had lifted me out of my marriage into the world, I had become sensitized to the issue of traditional divisions of domestic labor by reading sister Redstocking Pat Mainardi's satirical broadside "The Politics of Housework," then circulating in mimeograph (subsequently published in the 1970 collection *Notes from the Second Year*), which wittily detailed her mate's ploys for avoiding housework. That housework was up for political grabs, subject to maneuvering and negotiation, was only one of many previously unexamined premises of private life whose political bases were suddenly being exposed in the powerful light of feminist analysis. In a marriage complicated, unlike Mainardi's, by the presence of two impressionable children, I came to see domestic equity not only as simple justice but as one means of transforming society: by reforming the rearing of the young.[1]

Before the Marriage Agreement, I had been writing for over a year, having begun on the morning I dropped off my youngest child at nursery school, freeing me for three hours a day (actually two-and-a-half hours, after subtracting fifteen minutes to deliver her and fifteen minutes to collect her). I wrote secretly at first, fitting my writing into the cracks between domestic duties, thinking it too self-centered and pretentious an activity for one who had, as the times required, dutifully renounced personal ambition in favor of family life, and I sent out my stories under a pseudonym so that not even my husband (to whom I'd made the mistake of showing my first effort only to hear him declare it "a shambles") would know I was doing it. My earliest writings—a children's book (with one human character, a boy), three chapters of a never-finished family novel, a long letter-to-the-editor of the *Village Voice*, and several short stories, including one about a baby-sitter, another about an abortion, and finally one called "Traps," about a woman leaving her husband—were written before I found the movement; but as it was only a few months later that I began attending meetings, the two activities, writing and women's liberation, those twin threats to my marriage, are inextricably connected in my mind.

Like so many lives, mine began to change drastically as soon as I connected with the movement. Among the mostly childless women in both small groups I joined—Redstockings, which favored theory, and WITCH (Women's International Terrorist Conspiracy from Hell), which favored action—I was surprised to find myself suddenly valued for the very identity I had long felt ashamed of: for being a genuine stay-at-home housewife-mother. Those spunky young women, mostly in their twenties, treated me like a treasured resource instead of the useless has-been I considered myself at thirty-five, and I began to shed my diffidence—first in the group, then in my writing, though I prudently continued to hide from my husband the subversive nature of both. Even the marginal literary subject matter, female and domestic, to which I'd felt condemned by my limited experience, began to seem increasingly tenable subjects for fiction, and under cover of my pseudonym I started to submit my work to the new feminist journals suddenly springing up.

ALL AT ONCE, instead of finding humiliating rejection letters in my secret post office box I began to receive acceptances. Now there was an audience for "Traps," which appeared pseudonymously in the second issue (Winter 1970) of the feminist literary journal *Aphra* and eventually, in a slightly altered form, as the opening scene of my 1972 novel *Memoirs of an Ex-Prom Queen*. My first essay was a piece I volunteered to draft for my Redstockings group when someone pointed out that despite our extensive consciousness-raising on the topic of sex we had no sex article to hand out. Around the same time, through a contact with the (male) editor of a young-adult book series on "Women of America," I began a biography of the (then) forgotten anarchist Emma Goldman, whose works had all long been out of print. Based on my research I wrote essays on Goldman and on her sister anarchist Voltairine de Cleyre for the new *Women: A Journal of Liberation* (Spring and Fall issues, 1970), whose editors finally convinced me in the name of feminist courage to drop the pseudonym and sign my name.[2] Childless Goldman was impatient with women who remained in unhappy marriages, cavalierly asking (like certain Second-Wave feminists, whose gibes I sometimes fielded) why they didn't simply leave their husbands; to which de Cleyre, despite having refused on principle to marry the father of her own child, responded hotly: "Why don't you run when your feet are chained together? Why don't you cry out when a gag is on your lips? Why don't you raise your hands above your head when they are pinned fast to your sides?"—a disagreement in which I took a more than scholarly interest.[3] So much interest, in fact, that by the time I came to write my Marriage Agreement I had done sufficient brooding on "the marriage question"—and had developed enough feminist confidence—to dare to revise my life in light of it.

My impetus for the Agreement, which I intended as a critique of the inequities of both conventional marriage and divorce, was based on my own recent bizarre experience with divorce lawyers. (The first working title for the piece was actually "A Divorce Dilemma and a Marriage Agreement.") My ten-year-old (second) marriage had become increasingly shaky as my husband, the father of my children, preoccupied by a new business he'd opened in a neighboring state and a clandestine love affair he'd begun there, was spending so little time at home that I felt virtually abandoned. His betrayal particularly galled because in marrying him and starting a family I had myself renounced sexual adventure and quit my editorial job to accept as graciously as possible what I, as a 1950 graduate of white middle-class Cleveland Heights High School, took to be my fate. Feeling the press of time (thirty was then generally considered the outside age for having a first child; when I met my second husband I was twenty-six), I had struck with my husband the traditional, if unspoken, romantic deal: I would be the devoted wife and mother, he would be the family man, the good provider.

(I remember the moment—back before we had children—when I was first stung by the profound injustice of the arrangement. I was standing at the sink washing the dinner dishes when, as he often did, my husband approached me from behind, untied my apron strings, slipped his arms around my waist, and began kissing the back of my neck to lure me away from the sink; when I shook him off, objecting that I needed to finish the dishes, he turned me around, looked me over with an expression of such disenchantment I can see it still, and said in a voice full of sorrow how dull, how matronly I looked in an apron standing over a sinkful of dishes.)

Tied down by two small children, I had strenuously opposed his new business, knowing that it would take him away from us, but he had gone ahead with it anyway. In turn, when he'd opposed my testifying about my illegal abortions as risking his reputation, I'd defied his wishes. Now, humiliated and angry over his affair (with a woman more than twenty years his junior, whom he finally married many years later) and terrified that the children would be deprived of their father's physical, emotional, and financial support (the little money I earned by free-lance editing scarcely paid for the baby-sitter I hired a few hours a week), I fought back with all the strength I'd developed in the movement, soon taking a young lover of my own. The same feminist understanding and confidence that enabled me to stand up to my husband despite my dependence turned my love affair into a grand passion, complete with the orgasms I (like so many other heterosexual middle-class women of my generation, as we were discovering through consciousness-raising) had never experienced in fifteen years of marriage. Energized by my affair, bursting with sexual bravado, no wonder I volunteered to write the sex article for my Redstockings group. I titled the piece "Organs and Orgasms" and brazenly ended it with the admonition, "Think clitoris!"—one my husband, incensed by my admission that I'd long been faking orgasms, adamantly refused to heed.

Gradually our marital battle escalated, until at the end of each skirmish we were threatening one another with divorce grenades—now he would brandish the word, now I would, but in the end I was the bolder one. Or perhaps simply the more reckless. After all, what mere marriage could match the movement for excitement? Like other newly fledged feminists trying our wings, I was sometimes carried away by our own wishful rhetoric, soaring high into the clouds where feminism seemed invincible. Under the movement's spell we sometimes fancied raising our children together and growing old in joyful women's communities that would satisfy all our needs for companionship, sex, autonomy, power, and family, free of oppressive—or merely dull—marriages. Imagining women's autonomy, we demanded free, round-the-clock, universal child care and explored all sorts of alternatives to traditional marriage: free love, serial monogamy, lesbian partnerships, communal families, celibacy. Or we imagined ourselves as roving vigilante bands who through our indomitable solidarity would enforce our justice and wring compliance from men unable to live without us. For, contrary to media reports, women's liberation was not monolithically opposed to marriage. True, the group called The Feminists was against it, limiting to one-third of their membership women who lived with men, and Boston's Cell 16 was associated with a policy of celibacy; but my group, Redstockings, although sometimes divided on the issue, was concerned less with overthrowing the institution than with overhauling it to better serve women's interests by somehow forcing men to be more responsible mates and reliable fathers. Staying in the heterosexual arena to do close combat—planting, as it were, a subversive in every bed—was widely seen as a far more effective way to topple male supremacy than was any separatist path. Indeed, one triumph of the early movement was to make men responsible for child care at large movement gatherings.

Nevertheless, many women did extricate themselves from intolerable relationships, and many others raised their standards of the tolerable. But with two children to care for and a hefty rent, I always returned to the nest before dark. Though our marriage was strained to the breaking point, I could not bear the thought of our children fatherless. Despite our love affairs, neither my husband nor I really wanted divorce, with our children so young and our entire domestic establishment at stake—though I, emboldened by the power and thrill of the movement and at once bolstered and shaken by its critique of marriage, was more willing than he to pull the pin and lob the deadly weapon.

JUST AS MY HUSBAND AND I had once searched among obstetricians for one who would quietly agree not to breathe life into a seriously deformed newborn, so now, inspired by feminism, we searched among lawyers for one willing to draw up a radical separation agreement that would give us joint custody of our children. (We? Rather, *I* searched, dragging us off to one lawyer after another in hopes of devising the sort of innovative divorce that would somehow render my husband at once a dependable hands-on father and a civilized hands-off mate—as if divorce were simply marriage by other means.) In the late 1960s, however, it was not yet legally feasible to obtain joint custody in the State of New York. Although the idea had been explored experimentally in California, elsewhere it was still widely considered harmful to children for subjecting them to the vicissitudes of their parents' disputes and leaving them without a clear-cut line of authority. The first lawyer we went to, a smug, square-jawed traditionalist, literally laughed us out of his office—to my husband's relief and my fury. When we consulted movement lawyers, both leftist and (that newly emerging breed) feminist, whom I expected to be sympathetic to my ideas, they echoed the straight lawyer, warning us that if we didn't have a standard adversarial divorce we would be guilty of "collusion" and the divorce might not hold up (divorce by agreement was invalid, though all this would be changed by New York's 1975 divorce law reform); worse, if we insisted on joint custody, every time we had a disagreement or squabble the state would be free to step in and interfere, even, if it so chose, stripping us of custody of our children altogether. "Which is not so far-fetched, given your political activism," cautioned movement lawyer Carol Lefcourt. Acutely aware of the government's infiltration and subversion of the movement, I suddenly saw what folly it would be to invite Big Daddy into the heart of my family, no doubt to take the side of little daddy. Best not to marry at all, advised Lefcourt, but if married already, especially if there were children, safer not to be divorced.

Frustrated and fuming even as I laughed at these ludicrous legal conundrums, so oddly confirming of the anarchist case for having as little as possible to do with the state, I followed the lawyers' advice. Yet I could hardly fold my wings and meekly surrender to the status quo. If the law could not accommodate us, then why not sidestep it and design our own joint custody? In lieu of divorce, the finality of which terrified both me and my husband anyway, I decided to draft a private agreement to suit our needs. Instead of the unstated, conventionally gendered patriarchal rules we had unconsciously lived by before, I would formulate principles we could embrace consciously.

My husband, a large-minded but deeply traditional man, obligingly acquiesced—whether to ward off divorce, or out of conviction, or simply to humor me I'll never know. I do know that when I tried to involve him in thinking out our arrangement he took little interest. Perhaps he thought it trivial. Perhaps in the face of my relentless, to him fanatical, feminism he was merely practicing avoidance. Maybe he regarded the domestic concerns of such a document as outside his domain, despite our struggles. Or maybe he was just too preoccupied to be bothered. In any case, he left it to me. But then, why not? What had he to lose? With no sanction for the arrangement but our good will, if ultimately it didn't work out and shove came to slam or bam came to bolt, we could always hire two tough lawyers to slug it out.

IT WAS WITH FEMINIST IRONY, idealism, audacity, and glee that I sat down to compose my Marriage Agreement. Utilizing the methods of inquiry and self-examination I'd been developing through consciousness raising, I wrote down every task and detail of child care and housework I could think of, no matter how small, in order to discover and expose exactly what was involved in those trivial pursuits. Trivial? I'd show them trivial—and rub their noses in it!— from packing the children's lunches, taking them to the dentist, phoning around for a baby sitter, to cleaning, shopping, cooking, or stripping and remaking the beds. If these tasks were too insignificant to mention, then no father should mind doing them; and if some of them, like helping with homework, were as important as I thought or, like brushing their hair, as pleasurable, a father should treasure them. Having dropped out of Columbia's Ph.D. program in philosophy more than a dozen years before, it pleased me to apply my dormant analytical and critical skills to the minutiae of domestic management. The daughter of a lawyer, myself a lawyer manqué, I took special pleasure in the precision of the document.

The criticisms it later sparked centered mainly on the details, though I'd tried to make clear in my commentary that these would obviously vary from family to family, and that the schedule must be flexible, subject to frequent revision and renegotiation. As my good friend Jungian analyst Barbara Koltuv, who followed with a marriage agreement of her own, told a reporter, "Part of the reason for thinking out a contract is to find out what your problems are; it forces you to take charge of your life. Once you have the contract, you don't have to refer back to it. The process is what's important."[4] But to me, the soul of the Agreement—even more important than the process—was its founding principles.

*PART I. Principles.*

> 1. *We reject the notion that the work which brings in more money is more valuable. The ability to earn more money is a privilege which must not be compounded by enabling the larger earner to buy out of his/her duties and put the burden either on the partner who earns less or on another person hired from outside.* [5]

This principle went for the jugular of traditional marriage by challenging the basic rationalization of the division of labor in conventional nuclear families: money for services (which had been the unspoken basis of mine). To name earning power *privilege* was to challenge the very basis of value and strip the arrangement of its cover of justice. With what delight I penned that second sentence! And if it was unjust for "the larger earner to buy out of his/her duties and put the burden on the partner who earns less," then how comparably unjust must it be to put the burden on someone who earns still less. Let the man do his job, not buy out of it. Herein lay the Utopian core of the document, its challenge to class society, plumbing purposes deeper than domestic guidelines. In the long wake of this first principle must eventually come equitable pay, universal child care, class and gender justice.

2. *We believe that each partner has an equal right to his/ her own time, work, values, choices. As long as all duties are performed, each of us may use his/her extra time any way he/she chooses. If he/she wants to use it making money, fine. If he/she wants to spend it with spouse, fine. If not, fine.*

That last sentence was my code for sexual freedom, one of several messy subjects, including finances, I wasn't prepared to see muddy up the document. If this principle freed my husband to spend as much time as he liked in Pennsylvania as long as he pulled his weight at home, it also established my right, for the first time since I'd found the movement, to attend meetings as many nights as I chose without having to feel either negligent or guilty. It also gave me the right to go into my room and close the door to write, even with the children still awake or dirty dishes in the sink, when my husband was on duty. Quite a contrast to the way I'd felt as recently as 1967 when, on the eve of committing civil disobedience at a military induction center in protest against the Vietnam War, I'd begged my husband's indulgence (and, if necessary, bail money), knowing that if I were arrested I wouldn't get home in time to make dinner or get the children ready for school the next morning. And when my husband had tried to move us all to rural Pennsylvania to be near his work, I had felt willful and selfish refusing to go, knowing that a wife was supposed to follow her husband's job. No longer.

3. *As parents we believe we must share all responsibility for taking care of our children and home—not only the work but also the responsibility. At least during the first year of this agreement, sharing responsibility shall mean dividing the jobs and dividing the time.*

*In principle, jobs should be shared equally, 50-50, but deals may be made by mutual agreement . . . The schedule may be flexible, but changes must he formally agreed*

22

*upon. The terms of this agreement are rights and duties, not privileges and favors.*

After these *Principles* followed *PART II: Job Breakdown and Schedule*, detailing chores and tasks involved with *(A) Children* (Mornings, Transportation, Helping, Night-time, Baby Sitters, Sick Care, Weekends) and *(B) Housework* (Cooking, Shopping, Cleaning, Laundry).

The Agreement certainly upended the original basis of our marriage—and my husband often complained that I was changing the rules on him, just as I, seeing the family man I'd thought I'd married become a traveling man, accused him of changing the rules on me. Nevertheless, in good faith we both believed that reestablishing our relationship on an egalitarian basis was bound to improve it, freeing us from guilt and recriminations. I would no longer complain about his absence from the dinner table and he would no longer complain about my housekeeping. As it turned out, my husband, with higher standards of housekeeping than mine, did more cleaning than I. (A would-be bohemian, in my first marriage I had refused to own either a vacuum or a broom.) On my side, working as I did at home, I did more child care than he. But we genuinely tried for 50-50, even if our compliance was somewhat erratic.

A few months after we began following the Agreement, we were rewarded when one of our children memorably said, "You know, I used to love Mommy more, but now I love you both the same."

THAT REMARK SIGNALED TO ME that the time had come to write about and try to publish the Agreement. The first introduction I attempted told the divorce saga, complete with the ironies that had inspired me. But after a first draft I abandoned that strategy as tactless, introducing the document instead with a brief history of our domestic arrangements, pre-children and post-:

23

*When my husband and I were first married, a decade ago, keeping house was less a burden than a game. We both worked full time in New York City, so our small apartment stayed empty most of the day and taking care of it was very little trouble. Twice a month we'd spend Saturday cleaning and doing our laundry at the laundromat. We shopped for food together after work, and though I usually did the cooking, my husband was happy to help. Since our meals were simple and casual there were few dishes to wash. . . . Our domestic life was beautifully uncomplicated. When our son was born, our domestic life suddenly became quite complicated; and two years later, when our daughter was born, it became impossible. We automatically accepted the traditional sex roles that society assigns. . . .*

The article then goes on to describe the great changes and strains that overtook our marriage once I left my job to stay home with the children.

Entitled, simply, "A Marriage Agreement," the piece first appeared in the second issue of the new feminist journal *Up from Under* in August 1970. Over the next several years it was reprinted, with slight modifications, in such disparate magazines and books as *Redbook*, *New York* magazine, *Women's Liberation: A Blueprint for the Future*, the premiere issue of *Ms.*, *Life* magazine, and eventually—indeed, to this day—in many sociological, feminist, and legal textbooks and anthologies, including the standard casebook on contract law compiled by Harvard Law School's late Lon Fuller.

Like other feminist proposals, mine was initially greeted with wildly divergent responses: it was called liberating or stultifying, reasonable or cracked, lucid or legalistic, principled or petty. Despite the upheavals of the 1960s, the idea of shared child care and housework was then still widely considered unnatural and fatal to the male ego. And not only by traditionalists: in those days radical men, too, often felt justified in dismissing feminism as politically lame because of its concern for such distracting questions as who does the dishes. Even certain feminists, while agreeing with the principles of the Agreement, objected to its "legalistic" tone and purported rigidities. By the time of its apotheosis in a six-page spread in a 1972 *Life* magazine cover story, the Marriage Agreement was the subject of much debate in the popular press, where it was sometimes celebrated but more often derided by such antifeminist critics as Norman Mailer, Russell Baker, Joan Didion, and the infamous S. I. Hayakawa, who as president of San Francisco State College had summoned state troopers to suppress the 1968 student strike.

Even editors willing to publish it tried to subvert it. After it appeared in *Redbook* (under the editors' title "A Challenge to Every Marriage" and their cautious hedge that they found it "provocative"), more than two thousand letters poured in, one of the largest responses in *Redbook*'s history. I was heartened to find that though some readers were hostile, far more were supportive, and all but a few took the proposal seriously—hardly surprising, given *Redbook*'s predominantly housewife readership. But when I published my analysis of the two-thousand-plus letters in *Redbook* a year later (September 1972), I was appalled to find the editors going beyond a mere disclaimer in their headnotes to misrepresent my entire analysis. I had avoided using percentages in my article because so many of the most thoughtful letters were too complex to categorize readily, but no such scruples restrained the editors, who reported their own percentages of letters *for/against/undecided* (36/53/11) as if they were mine, and edited my key paragraph to make it appear that I agreed with them. I immediately protested such highhanded treatment and reluctantly gave my own, very different summary figures (60/30/10) in a long letter that was eventually printed on the letters page over an editorial apology.

STILL, CONTROVERSY WAS EXACTLY WHAT I wanted. I remember the mounting excitement with which I read Mailer's notorious 1971 attack on feminism, *The Prisoner of Sex*, as it was first serialized in *Harper's*—the same excitement with which I had once relished philosophical debate, the subtleties of law, and sexual adventure but had traded for family life. As I came to his concluding section, which opened by quoting in full the Principles of my Marriage Agreement, I exulted over having hit the mark. "No, he would not be married to such a woman," wrote Mailer of himself in the third person. "If he were obliged to have a roommate, he would pick a man. The question [with which he began his inquiry: Who finally would do the dishes?] had been answered. He could love a woman and she might even sprain her back before a hundred sinks of dishes in a month, but he would not be happy to help her if his work should suffer, no, not unless her work was as valuable as his own." Oh, exquisite triumph! The first principle of my Agreement, that a woman's work was by definition as valuable as a man's—indeed, that the comparison was henceforth impermissible, not least because absent the opportunity that must follow domestic equality no one could know what women might do—this, Mailer could not swallow.

Perhaps it was the Agreement's very reasonableness that made it seem so threatening, transgressive, outrageous to men like Mailer. In fact, that tantalizing combination of reasonable and outrageous that colors so much early Second-Wave feminist writing may account for the wide range of reader response. For though I certainly meant my proposal in earnest, I also relished the ironic face with which I presented it: a sardonic lift of eyebrow as I laid out the principles, a curl of the lip as I listed the tasks in excruciating detail, a wicked chortle as I mocked man's self-importance as a mere ruse for getting out of doing the dishes. The Agreement became another of those sly inside jokes, so common in those days, that knowing women crowed over together but that many men just didn't get—or perhaps, being their butts, got only too well.[6]

Though in his footnote to my article Mailer had carelessly cited *Off Our Backs* instead of *Up From Under* and had misspelled my last name with an *Sch*, at least he got the title right. Not so, many another, who persistently referred to the Agreement as a Contract. Perhaps the mistake was set in motion by the inclusion of the Agreement (under its correct name) in a sidebar in Susan Edmiston's provocative essay, "How to Write Your Own Marriage Contract," published in the premier issue of *Ms*; but when the error took on a life of its own despite my repeated objections, I could hardly avoid concluding there were political motives at work. *Agreement* sounds amicable and voluntary, whereas *contract* sounds adversarial and legal. Our arrangement, which we had established in part precisely to escape the law, had no legal status or intention; we simply wanted to divide up the duties for our own education and convenience, to improve things at home. Yet how easy to undermine our simple idea by substituting one word for another. Does this sound far-fetched? Consider: though I granted permission to Hayakawa to quote from my article only on condition that he use the word *agreement* instead of *contract* and even saw corrected galleys that met my condition before I sent in my written permission, in the finished book there was *contract* back in place in every instance where it had been changed to *agreement* in the galleys. Consider: though I got *Life*'s firm promise to use my title before I granted permission or signed a release, *Life* got around the restriction by using a huge one-word title, "CONTRACT," on one page opposite a sentence describing it on the facing page, in letters a fraction the size, as "A 50-50 Marriage Agreement." In the table of contents *Life* used the title "Living by Contract"; and on the cover, beneath a small photo of my husband and me— one of four pictured examples of "Marriage Experiments" that included: "Unmarried Parents in a Boston Suburb," a "Collective Family in a Big House in Berkeley," and a "Frontier Partnership in Idaho"—appeared the caption "Work-sharing Contract in New York," with no mention of *agreement* at all. Perhaps a mainstream journal like *Life* must inevitably try to tame and depoliticize everything between its covers: in the galleys of the article, the reporter, Patricia Coffin, had me spending my free time at art galleries instead of at political rallies. When I objected to this falsification it was corrected, but the offending *contract* remained.

Still, under whatever title, that *Life* coverage did help to get people thinking about alternatives to conventional marriage, including the controversial idea of domestic equality—so well, in fact, that when the magazine decided to do a follow-up of the major stories of the year for their late-December wrap-up issue, their April 28 report on "The Marriage Experiments" was among those selected. Good for the movement—but for one hitch: when Pat Coffin called to set up another interview, I had to tell her that my husband was on the West Coast and couldn't be reached.

What I didn't tell her was that, his business having recently folded, he had followed his young lover, then a student at Berkeley, to California. We had separated only months after our Marriage Agreement's appearance in *Life*. Much had happened to us in those brief months, including the nearly simultaneous publication of my first novel and collapse of my husband's business— events that together loosened our ties; but *Life* readers, ignorant of our private history, and not knowing that our Marriage Agreement was by then three years old, could easily presume a causal connection between the Agreement and our precipitous separation. Thinking of the fun Mailer and the others could have with the news of our breakup if they got wind of it, I dreaded an exposé—particularly when Pat Coffin suggested that perhaps she could interview each of us separately. I managed to put her off by fudging my husband's address, but I was terrified she would somehow discover his whereabouts.

When *Life* unexpectedly announced to the world that it would be folding before the end of the year, I was jubilant. Indeed, so powerfully did I feel the swelling force of the movement that I wondered if perhaps it wasn't my personal feminist genie that had delivered *Life* its death blow to save face for me and the movement. (Just as, following the signing of a book contract some months earlier, I'd suspected my genie of exterminating the editor who had laid a hand suggestively on my knee, and would again some months later suspect her of conveniently delivering back to me my compromising love letters only hours before my lover's fatal heart attack. Oh, the power of the movement!)

I REALIZE THIS CONFESSION MAY be construed in some quarters as feeding the notion that feminism destroys marriages—a charge akin to the one that feminism destroys fetuses. In that feminism offers women the possibility of autonomy, giving us permission to leave a bad marriage or terminate an unwanted pregnancy, both accusations are partially true. Before feminism, divorce, like abortion, was often regarded as scandalous; until the 1970s, in many states the only ground for divorce was (criminal) adultery, the only ground for abortion threat to the mother's life, while now, thanks in part to the women's movement, divorce and abortion are widely accepted as basic rights. But that's only part of the story. As I once pointed out to a man who accused me of having caused his wife to run off with the baby after reading one of my novels, *he* may have had something to do with it, too. True, a few women, torn by ambivalence and carried away by movement rhetoric that seemed at times to condemn all marriages (and families) as oppressive, committed acts they later regretted—ending relationships, postponing pregnancies, leaving children—only to change their minds after it was too late. But many others acted without regret and some like me struggled in the name of feminism to improve family life by making it more equitable, flexible, and thus viable. As I wrote for a "Symposium on Marriage" in the feminist literary journal *Aphra* (Fall 1973—before New York reformed its divorce law): "Children will continue to be born and reared. Adults may fairly be expected to make sacrifices for them. Marriage insures that women will not be the only ones to make those sacrifices." My feminist intent was neither to bring down nor to shore up marriage but to improve women's lot within and without it.

Now, many years after my second divorce, looking back across a quarter century of social change to try to recover the feelings that led to my Marriage Agreement, I wonder if writing it was an act of political imagination, personal conciliation, or feminist revenge. I do remember the elation with which I wrote it; and I also remember that later, as I read letter after wistful letter from *Redbook* readers applauding the Agreement and envying me my "understanding husband" or begging for the secret of how I managed to get him to go along with it, I sensed an uncomfortable disparity between my power and theirs. It was not only that I had privileges many of them didn't share, like rewarding remunerative work and no more toddlers at home. At that point, unlike most of them isolated in their disappointing marriages, I, fueled by feminist insight, anger, and pride, felt the power of a burgeoning movement backing me. The unspoken sanction for my Agreement, the secret force behind it (and a reason, perhaps, to call it a contract after all?) was my bottom-line willingness to divorce him if he wouldn't agree. I puzzled over the effect on the movement of admitting this straight out: would it help or hurt the cause?—help it by revealing the necessity of struggle, good will notwithstanding, or hurt it by exposing the all-but-prohibitive stakes? And later, as it became increasingly clear that our Agreement did not really "work" despite our best intentions—that, since my husband's work took him so often out of town, I continued to do most of the parenting (and gladly, too, knowing how much calmer and freer we each felt during our long stretches apart), and for the same reason, by default as it were, he let the housework slide, and eventually our marriage, like so many, foundered—I wondered which was better for the movement, particularly in face of the conservative attacks: to hide these failings or confess them? But why, I wonder now, should the "failure" of my marriage, or any marriage, have seemed to me so potentially embarrassing for the movement—any more than the cancer death of food-reformer Adele Davis should have so scandalized the health-food movement? As if a person, or a marriage, should be immortal, or as if our marital breakdown must be laid at the door of our singular Agreement rather than of our accumulating disagreements. When dozens of feminist activists, myself included, had staged a sit-in on March 18, 1970, at the editorial offices of that bulwark of traditional gender roles, the *Ladies' Home Journal*, to demand a platform in its pages for feminist ideas, one of the reasons we selected that magazine was to challenge its famous monthly column, "Can This Marriage Be Saved?" (which Redstockings member Ellen Willis proposed retitling "Can This Marriage"). Yet, despite that action, two years later I evidently still thought it my duty to shield *Life*'s audience from the truth about my own marriage, as if the point were to save it.

THE TRUTH? LIKE EVERY IDEAL, our Marriage Agreement fell far short of the standard it proposed, indeed, it failed. Worse, its failure was as emblematic as it was personal: in the absence of economic equality and/or a strong movement, decades after women's liberation launched the battle over housework, married men in the United States still do precious little domestic labor—only 10 percent more than they did two decades earlier, according to one survey. *The Second Shift* (Viking, 1989), Arlie Hochschild's important study of divisions of domestic chores among married, predominantly middle-class working couples in families with young children, reports that what the women's movement began is now a "stalled revolution": only 18 percent of the husbands in the study did half the housework, 21 percent did a moderate amount, and 61 percent still did little or none, though their wives held down outside jobs. And even among couples who share more equitably in the work at home, "women do two-thirds of the *daily* jobs, like cooking and cleaning up—jobs that fix them into a rigid routine," while men do less-frequent tasks like fixing appliances or changing the oil in the family car. *Families on the Faultline* (HarperCollins, 1994), Lillian B. Rubin's recent examination of working-class families, shows that many working-class men who would not even pay lip service to gender equality two decades ago are now "quite sensitive to the needs and wishes of their wives"; yet because they fail to translate this sensitivity into action, the housework question is now often "a wrenching source of conflict."[7] The exception, writes Rubin, is in black families: "Black men are the most likely to be real participants in the daily life of the family and are more intimately involved in raising their children than any of the others. . . . Compared to their white, Asian, or Latino counterparts, the black families look like models of egalitarianism. Nearly three quarters of the men in the African-American families in this study do a substantial amount of the cooking, cleaning, and child care, sometimes even more than their wives." According to Hochschild, "the most important injury" to women in unequal marriages is not the unfair leisure gap between the sexes, not women's exhaustion from the double day, but rather that they "carry into their marriage the distasteful and unwieldy burden of resenting their husbands."

Conflict, discontent, resentment: a bitter legacy. And with consciousness changing so much faster than practice, and far more on the part of women than of men, discontent and resentment must be at record highs. Hard on the children (like our own, who unfortunately were spared none of the hardships of growing up in an embattled household; for after that first separation my husband and I got back together and remained married until the children were grown); hard on everyone involved. Still, an improvement over the cavalier dismissal of housework as "trivial," and better by far than the unconscious, pre-feminist alternatives, which, in any case, have become increasingly untenable now that most women, regardless of class, race, or age of children, hold down outside jobs.

Yes, our Marriage Agreement failed, and our marriage after it. But the unbearable status quo, to challenge which I had written the Agreement in the first place, also collapsed—fell in a whirling freefall that, like so many Utopian fictions and experiments, landed us somewhere we never imagined. Once the feminist challenge pushed open the door on traditional marriage and took a good look inside, it could not be the same again. Even though the goal of domestic equality between cohabiting parents is honored—like the marriage vows themselves—mainly in the breach, at least it is now a commonplace, no longer an outrage. Despite the gloomy news on actual housework done, the *ideal* of egalitarian marriage has steadily grown (espoused by 48 percent of the wives in Hochschild's study, if only by 20 percent of the husbands), that of traditional gender roles within marriage has steadily shrunk (down to 12 percent of the wives and 18 percent of the husbands), and the rest (40 percent of the wives and 62 percent of the husbands) are somewhere "in transition."

PARENTING IS STILL profoundly gendered, and the nuclear family is still the setting vastly preferred for child-rearing, but in fact fewer and fewer children grow up in a traditional household or even one where both biological parents reside. Instead, to accommodate paternal flight or enact eternal hope, there has been an irrepressible proliferation of new de facto forms of family life—from jumbled, blended, divorce-extended families to single-parent, lesbian or gay domestic partnerships, and even the occasional innovative experiment. In a May 14, 1994, column in the *New York Times*, Peter Steinfels proposed a "thought experiment" doing away with legal marriage altogether: "The state would have nothing to do with it. The whole business would be strictly a private agreement. . . . The only thing that would be essential is that the couple—or the triad or the quintet—agree freely. . . . The number, the sex, the hierarchy or permanence of spouses in any household would be no more a matter of legal requirement—or ultimately, of social concern—than the number or size of the rooms."[14]

Such proliferation ensures that even in the face of punishing institutional biases that restrict nontraditional families' rights, traditional hierarchical marriage will not again be monolithically entrenched. But it does nothing to correct or even address the gendered division of labor that permeates our society. It is this domestic inequality, not the form or legitimacy of marriage, that continues to worry me. Not that I don't have a cheer for every imaginative or brave attempt. But the inevitable slippage between intentions and their outcomes, particularly in the absence of a strong feminist movement, keeps me asking cautiously of each, Who will benefit, who will lose, and who will wind up with the housework?

Still, as an incurable movement person, for all my skepticism I can't help hoping that if attitudes keep on changing at the rate they have, then maybe, just maybe, in another twenty years . . .

## NOTES

1. In the following decade this would be a major thrust of Dorothy Dinnerstein's *The Mermaid and the Minotaur* (Harper & Row, 1976), Adrienne Rich's *Of Woman Born* (Norton, 1976), and Nancy Chodorow's *The Reproduction of Mothering* (University of California Press, 1978), among other feminist analyses of the family.

2. Ardent feminist though I was, my consciousness changed slowly. Except for the story "Traps," published under my pseudonym, all my early writings were signed with my married name, Alix Shulman; not until 1972, just before publication of my first novel, did it occur to me to reclaim my maiden name, Kates, even though I had for several years been cheering the work of such self-named feminists as Kathie Sarachild, Betsy Warrior, and Laura X. Since by that time I had already published three children's books, two edited collections, and one biography all under the name Alix Shulman, I felt it would be imprudent to switch midstream to my maiden name, Kates, so I compromised by inserting it in the middle. But I've often regretted that I didn't drop my married name then. When I was finally divorced in 1985 I tried to drop Shulman in my private life—but even then I wondered how my children would feel seeing me shed their name.

3. When feminist friends occasionally directed the same question to me, asking, "When are you going to leave that husband?" I regularly quipped back, "Not until you're ready to take care of my kids."

4. Susan Edminston, "How to Write Your Own Marriage Contract," *New York* magazine, December 20, 1971.

5. This and the following excerpts are taken from the version published in *Redbook*, August 1971.

6. Several years later I met Mailer at a book party for a children's anthology to which we had each contributed a story and introduced myself as the author of the Marriage Agreement. NM: That was a dumb idea. AKS: Only if you didn't get it. NM: You mean it was supposed to be ironic? I missed that. AKS (throwing Mailer's own familiar slur back at him): That's because you antifeminists have no sense of humor. NM (pausing to scratch his head, as he fails again to get it): Hmm. That's what I always say about you feminists.

7. Rubin notes that housework more than child care is at issue in these families, "for despite the enormous ferment in family life over these last decades, the cultural definition of the good parent has changed little. Parenting . . . remains woman's work. It's mother who's still held accountable for [the children's] moral development, their emotional stability, and their worldly success or failure. Father need only make a living for them to satisfy his part of the bargain. Any unanticipated ripple in the children's development is quite simply mom's failure."

# COMMUNICATION BETWEEN THE SEXES: BREAKING THE TRUCE

AMONG THE MORE STARTLING CHANGES that have occurred in communications in the last decade are the changes between what women and men are telling each other and hearing, how they are speaking among themselves, what they are leaving unsaid.

About fifteen years ago, the truce that had prevailed between the sexes since the end of World War II began to break down, and open rebellion broke out among women, gradually causing deep changes in the way people understand the relations between men and women. The rebellion began in the United States, but soon it spread throughout the world, provoking a strong counterattack, until by now changes have been launched in our consciousness of gender, and of how men and women think about themselves and each other, which constitute a truly international social movement.

Today I want to talk about some of the changes, as I see them. But first I'd like to acknowledge that although I am speaking about men and women in general, I realize that there are only individual lives, which means there must be many exceptions—maybe only exceptions—as there are whenever one tries to characterize or describe any large group, whether it be a generation, an era, an age group, a nation, a region, a subculture, a class. Even so, I think it's possible and useful to attempt to discover patterns despite all those exceptions who, like certain civilians in a modern war seemingly oblivious of the news, will nevertheless find themselves deeply affected by the action at the front.

As a feminist, who has spent much of the last fifteen years writing about relations between the sexes, I know that this subject, discussed in mixed company, sometimes has the effect of making the speaker's opinions, however straightforward and honestly stated, seem antagonistic, which in turn may provoke a defensive response or hostile counterattack. This is what happens in a quarrel: each side imagines that the other is distorting the truth in order to undermine or beat the opponent. One of the first things that happens in battle is that communications between the opposing sides break down. This poses a problem for anyone wanting to speak openly about a contested subject. I want to assure you that I am not interested today in furthering a battle. I simply want to speak my honest opinions and describe some things I've observed. I want to issue a sort of dispatch from the front as I see it. Each one of us could probably issue such a dispatch, since we all live in some sort of balance, however precarious, with the opposite sex; and since the current phase of the battle of the sexes—that is, the current rebellion of women—is being conducted on a great many different fronts, with some defeats and some victories, our reports might bear little resemblance to each other.

And communication, remember, can include not only the truth but also a great deal of untruth, even of deceit. Communication may usually be undertaken to convey opinion or knowledge, but it may also be for other purposes, too: to conceal, to manipulate, to convince, to injure, to move, to sway. Such motives have always been an essential part of communication between the sexes, where so much of our emotional life is conducted. The traditions and clichés of our culture, beginning with Eve, would have it that women are the world's great deceivers and manipulators. And since the huge power disparity between men and women historically left women with little power but that of personal charm, manipulation was one of the few effective weapons available to them for defending themselves against the overwhelming power of men. When women had no rights, retaining the patronage of a man was a matter of survival, and it was only sensible to use any means and every artifice to do so.

A modern acknowledgement of this approach to sexual relations is exemplified by the highly successful program of Marybelle Morgan's Total Woman, an approach, by the way that many men applaud and appreciate. I think the reason for its success with women is its realism, its realpolitik, its acknowledgement that there is still a great power disparity between the sexes. As women gained rights, their dependency on manipulation diminished, and deceit became increasingly mutual or reciprocal, despite the patriarchal tradition that continues to see women as the manipulators. Women's literature and the whole tradition of the seduced and abandoned woman testify to the role of the male deceiver. In the nineteenth century, when women came to be seen as the civilizers and guardians of virtue, men banded together to avoid and deceive them as the enemies of pleasure. Men's clubs fostered that end which, in other forms, persists today. I recently read about a bar in Atlanta where there is a special telephone booth called the Excuse Booth, equipped with recordings of various background noises that bar patrons may play when phoning home with an alibi. Still, of the two polar modes of communication between the sexes, manipulation and honesty, it is hard to say which is the more authentic. For with power between the sexes still vastly unequal and with women economically dependent on men, it is self-deceiving to pretend otherwise; to act as if equality prevailed, as if gender differences were insignificant is as dishonest as the more traditional deceptions, and in some situations is foolish besides. The fact is, hardly anyone is gender blind; it is practically impossible to face someone of the other sex without a pervasive consciousness of sex and difference. It's always there in the air between a man and a woman, whatever their sexual orientation.

Communication between the sexes is further complicated by the fact that despite the so-called sexual revolution of recent years, sexual relations are shrouded in mystery, secrecy and shame. People have different ways of adapting to the givens of their lives. For the sake of peace, or because of the distribution of power, people often leave unsaid some of the things they know clearly, while other things, only vaguely perceived and imperfectly known, remain hidden even from themselves. But in times of sudden or rapid change, when new possibilities fill the air and what was taken as given suddenly no longer seems so inevitable—at such times the veils of secrecy may be torn off and the hidden brought to light and named. This is what seems to me to have happened between the sexes in the past decade or so.

# 2

I HAVE SPOKEN OF A rebellion among women and of a broken truce. Let me describe them. I think the truce that prevailed between the sexes in the two decades from the end of World War II (when women who had been wartime workers were required to give their jobs back to men) till the mid-1960s rested on an agreement that women would not complain of injustice, would accept the prevailing distribution of power in society between the sexes, would content themselves with their supportive, service role, their subordination to men, in exchange for security, peace, and (if I may use the word) love. The fact that women were not content, often had only the most tenuous security, and were as much despised or feared as loved, remained an unspoken, even shameful, secret. The rebellion, the breaking of that truce, consisted first of all in telling the secrets, speaking forbidden thoughts, in complaining if you will—at first in small groups of mainly young women getting together among themselves, and soon after, loudly, publicly, widely, fearlessly. The women kicked off their rebellion by demanding justice and a voice. Immediately, the voice: the right to speak and be listened to; and for the future, justice: in the words of Susan B. Anthony, "Men their rights and nothing more, women their rights and nothing less."

Thus, the very earliest organized public actions of the women's liberation movement were called "speak-outs" in which the taboo broken was, precisely, the taboo against certain kinds of speech. The first speak-out was on abortion, in which women broke a very strong and longstanding taboo, one which had the sanction of law behind it, by publicly admitting to having had illegal abortions and describing the painful feelings and terrifying circumstances in which they occurred. Next was a speak-out on rape (and some of you will remember when for a woman to admit to having been raped was more dangerous and demeaning to her, the victim, than to the perpetrator); and soon after that came speak-outs on most of the issues that have become familiar to us as "women's issues": economic discrimination, the ghettoizing of mothers, sexual abuse and harassment, violence against women, the sexual double standard, unjust marriage and divorce laws, you can extend the list yourselves.

And the socks. Socks and housework. Women suddenly felt free to complain about the socks men left on the floor to be picked up. And although men immediately dismissed socks and housework as a trivial issue, it became and is still one of the focal points of resentment between the sexes. A newly issued report, by sociologists Phillip Blumstein and Pepper Schwartz, sponsored by the National Science Foundation, the largest study of couples ever undertaken, reports that housework is still one of the touchiest issues between couples. Not only traditional marriages but new marriages and cohabiting relationships were more likely to fail if the man felt his partner did not do her fair share of the housework—which meant practically all of it; but when a woman felt her partner did not do his share, the relationship was not threatened.

It's not that women had been silent until then, although throughout history various male philosophers have argued that women are, or at least ought to be, silent. But women's talk and their confidences to each other were denigrated as gossip, their concerns—personal and domestic—considered trivial. This double standard of speech goes back to the Greeks at least. A few examples will do:

Sophocles: "Silence gives the proper grace to women."

Samuel Johnson: "A woman preaching is like a dog's walking on his hind legs. It is not done well, but you are surprised to find it done at all."

Nietzsche: "When a woman inclines to learning there is usually something wrong with her sex apparatus."

Malcolm X: "To tell a woman not to talk too much was like telling Jesse James not to carry a gun, or telling a hen not to cackle. Can you imagine Jesse James without a gun, or a hen that didn't cackle?"

Some modern scholars argue that men and women have what seem in some ways to amount to two different cultures, including their speech. This is no surprise. Since boy and girl children are treated differently, since the two sexes are raised in somewhat different worlds and therefore experience reality differently, naturally, their expression of reality in language and culture is bound to be different. Most of the studies of men's and women's speech over the last decade confirm that men and women have different styles of speech, different common subjects, different ways of conveying meaning; many key words and concepts have somewhat different meanings on women's lips than on men's and mean different things when applied to women than they mean when applied to men. Study after study comes up with the same results: men speak more loudly than women, more often than women, are more apt to interrupt, impose their views, and take over the conversation than women. Now, isn't this interesting? The patriarchal cliché of our culture has it that women are the blabbermouths who never shut up. But the studies consistently show the opposite. They show that women tend to smile more, be more supportive in conversation, ask encouraging questions, provide conversational openings. In mixed company men tend to dominate in speech as in the rest of public life; women remain good listeners. To anyone who has been in mixed classes of men and women none of this is news, especially in contrast to what goes on in all-woman classes. And these differences in speech are evident very early in life; by five years old the speech patterns of boys and girls are recognizably different.

Of course, men and women understand each other's language. But often they understand the words and concepts they hear in their own way, rather than the way the other is using them. A couple of examples will do. I have just returned from half a year on a small island in Maine where I lived alone in a house on a point surrounded by ocean with no plumbing, electricity, telephone, or even a road. Perfectly isolated. People who visited me all remarked that in my place, they would be afraid, afraid to be there all alone; but the men and women had entirely different images of what was frightening there. To the women, the terror was of what I can only call "the man"—the bogie man, the crazed intruder, the sex maniac. This fear response was provoked by any unknown male coming across the beach, and especially at night, by any unidentified sound, however slight. None of the men expressed these fears. Instead, the men said they would be afraid of falling on the rocks and breaking a leg or otherwise injuring themselves in such a way that they would be incapacitated, unable to get help, without anyone to help or take care of them. None of them were afraid of noises or intruders. Fear meant different things to the men and to the women.

Another example is illustrated in a joke that was going around last year, one that perhaps not all of you will even get. A man comes home from work to find his wife lying on the sofa, sick. He says to her, don't worry darling, I'll get the dinner tonight. She thanks him gratefully, and closes her eyes while he goes off to the kitchen. After a while he returns, puzzled. Excuse me, honey, he says, I went into the kitchen to get the dinner, but I can't seem to find it. Where do you keep it?

A case might be made that such concepts as love, happiness,

achievement, aggression—the list could go on and on—commonly mean somewhat different things for men and for women, reflecting their different worlds of experience—different enough to sometimes cause real misunderstandings.

Now, when one nation conquers another, often one of the first things done is official suppression of the language of the conquered. So the language becomes a symbol of the tension and a vital force of resistance. Suppressed people speak in codes, metaphors, stories. Their literature expresses the hidden life of the people to each other over the heads and ears of the conquerors. I'm not proposing that women have been like a conquered nation, but I am suggesting that during the time of their rebellion certain words they used among themselves assumed a vitality and symbolic status analogous to those of a people resisting conquest. The earliest women's liberation groups took for themselves such despised names as Witch and Bitch; the largest most successful feminist publishing house in England is called Virago.

During the rebellion, what was new was women's sudden insistence that their concerns were not trivial but important, that what seemed like personal complaints were at their very core political and far too important to keep politely secret any longer or to allow to be dismissed as gossip. The birth of the so-called gender gap that is now emerging as a major factor in national politics occurred when women decided to express their differences with men in public. The differences had long been there, of course, but as long as women were persuaded or intimidated into keeping those differences private, they could not become significant issues in politics.

Suddenly, women asked to be listened to, acknowledged, taken seriously by men—and not simply on matters men had agreed were significant but on matters of central concern to women. Women, at least educated women, had long been listening to men's opinions and studying their culture; now women wanted men to hear their side. However, the main responses of men, with a few treasured exceptions, were at first either to laugh and dismiss women's complaints yet again, or else to feel shocked, betrayed, threatened, angry—so that almost from the start, this great outpouring of women's speech, this epidemic taboo breaking, this new exposing of secrets occurred almost exclusively between women: woman to woman. Most men were not, are still not, particularly interested to hear what these women were saying. The results of a decade of brilliant women's scholarship, for instance, restoring to history some record of women's lives and work, are seldom integrated into the standard school and college curricula; instead, women's studies are a ghetto few men enter; most men remain unaware of their own sexist bias and speech, or worse, continue to use it despite their awareness—*The New York Times*, for example, absolutely refuses to use the marriage-neutral honorific Ms., even when the women they interview insist upon it. The heartening new non-sexist version of the Bible adopted recently by the National Council of Churches is evidently meeting a great deal of resistance.

Nevertheless—and this is the other important and promising change I've observed in communication between the sexes—there are signs that some of what women have been saying may have started getting through to men. Not necessarily because of the strength of women's arguments, for although women's reasons for demanding justice, equality, autonomy seem to me unassailable, I believe that people usually hear what they want to hear and have no trouble rationalizing their own self interest. No, if women are getting through to men, it is because there is something that women now have that men sense they may need and want. Since women began speaking out together and tearing off those veils of secrecy and shame, it has become apparent to many observers that women are the ones whose lives seem most full of new possibilities now; with their new consciousness of possibility, theirs are the lives which seem inspired by hope and imagination. On today's campuses, where there is reputedly a depressing passivity and morose apathy among the student body, women in groups often defy that description. The vitality and vivacity, the insight and vision that have come to characterize the new speech of women together is in some places so evident and even inspiring that perhaps for the first time, at least since the culmination of the first wave of feminism in the women's suffrage amendment, some men are feeling a desire to find out what's been going on among women and, fearing to be left out, may actually believe they have something important to learn from women, may even secretly envy them. Men, looking at these women nowadays, may envy them not only their vitality but their ease of intimacy, their comfort with each other and with their feelings.

Let me make it clear that the changes I'm talking about are not changes in power relations between the sexes; I think that actually very little has been accomplished in that regard. Observe, for example, that women in this country still make only 60 cents for every dollar men make despite the affirmative action laws, the lawsuits, the massive entry of women into the paid work force, the changed consciousness, the token elevations of women. No, I am talking only about a change in awareness—always the first step to structural change. I am amazed at how much awareness has changed in a mere fifteen years. And what strikes me as the most amazing change in communications between the sexes is precisely this: that men may be starting to listen to women's talk. I don't have much evidence, but I'm certainly encouraged by the awards of Pulitzer Prizes to women writing about women: last year in drama to Marsha Norman for *Night Mother,* and this year in fiction to Alice Walker for *The Color Purple.* Women getting occasional prestigious awards is not new, but receiving awards for writing almost exclusively about women's experience is, I think, something new.

This is not only because women together are hopeful or are visibly turning their lives around without help from men. It is also, I think, because the kinds of power and knowledge that men have traditionally wielded to control and transform the world is fast becoming counterproductive. The great technological achievements over which men have presided for hundreds of years are out of control, threatening to crash: resources are growing increasingly scarce, pollution is tainting the planet, and bigger is no longer better. Another style, another sort of technology, another approach has got to be tried. And traditionally, women, who have been excluded from the big, corporate, competitive, aggressive, scientific technologically heavy enterprise, have had to develop other means to get what they need. Whereas in the past, it was women's speech and knowledge, gestures and style, concerns and obsessions that were widely discredited, now, because of the plight we are all in, it is patriarchal speech, style, stance, obsessions that are coming increasingly under question and in some quarters are beginning to be discredited. The man-talk of men among themselves, in the past considered privileged and precious to the same extent that women's talk was discounted, now seems increasingly inadequate to quite a few men themselves, including young ones, and in increasing numbers. And that seems to me new and significant.

I believe there is nothing inevitable about the gender divisions that have been enforced and reinforced by culture, but they do run deep. In some ways, in fact, they may have been deepened by the breaking of the truce. It's ironic that a movement initially undertaken to step up communications by ending a long silence had as one of its earliest consequences an almost opposite result: communications broke down. As I've said, this is what usually happens in a quarrel. When women began talking openly among themselves, to a certain extent they stopped listening to men. They were no longer willing to be interrupted or to have men's views imposed upon them. This is why they did not invite men to their meetings. In the interests of truth, they deliberately rejected the tracts written by men that passed for knowledge about women—about women's psychology, their capabilities, their desires, their bodies, their sexuality, their place—and instead set out to make their own investigations and draw their own conclusions about themselves. Thus women's studies was born. At the same time, they also seemed to be talking less to men—partly because a lot of women got very busy: going back to school, going out to new jobs, going to meetings, but also because when men refused to listen, now, instead of cajoling or smiling or accommodating them, a lot of women dared simply to ignore them. In their non-verbal communications too, in some respects the sexes grew farther apart when the truce was broken. One of the great taboo subjects women began to discuss was sex itself, their satisfactions and disappointments, their pleasures and fears. One of the first rights newly daring women claimed for themselves was the right to say no to their husbands and lovers, without guilt, about having sex, as well as the right to have no less sexual freedom than men. With autonomy one of women's most longed for goals, in increasing numbers women began to envision the possibility of a fulfilling life without necessarily getting or staying married. The divorce rate soared, and in a parallel movement among men as well as women, homosexuality surfaced as a legitimate and preferred way of living. The changes in consciousness I'm talking about, however, are not restricted to the young, the urbane, the radical, the feminist. They are much more widespread. Evidence is everywhere, but I'll just tell you about one conversation I overheard on a ferryboat going from an island in Maine to Portland a few weeks ago. These islanders are mostly lobstering people, fishermen and their families, mostly conservative, individualistic Yankees. Two women, senior citizens and clearly local people, were sitting behind me talking about the divorce of one of their children. I'm going to give you the whole conversation, verbatim, as I took it down while they spoke.

*"Let's face it," said one, "we've put up with a lot of guff they wouldn't put up with anymore."*
   *"Damn right," said the other. [PAUSE]*
   *"We still do."*
   *"You betcha."*
   *"Better than being alone, though."*
   *"That's the choice, I'm afraid."*
   *"I don't know, though. Now they've got those senior citizen*

*organizations, they get together and have a ball. Don't even need
a husband anymore."*
      *"Long as you can take care of yourself."*
      *"Long as you can afford it."*

I doubt that this conversation could have occurred until recently.
Through most of our history, men, who have had something
of a monopoly on the creation of official knowledge, as well as on
power, have seldom felt the need to listen to what women say or to
learn what women know from the experience of their very different
lives. Women's literature was not taught, women's history was not
recorded, women's insights, methods, speech, were not valued. This
is what may perhaps finally be starting to change. Let's hope so.

# SEX

# THE WAR IN THE BACK SEAT

THE REVIVAL OF THE 1940s and 1950s is upon us. That Middle-American time of my youth is gaining its place in our historical imagination. Movies, essays, stories, novels, and the sheer passage of time have already begun transforming that era from banal to exotic. The record is being filled not only with nostalgia but with critical insight, as writing men of wit try to pin down those days. Nevertheless, something crucial is missing from the record. For the reality being recorded about that era is essentially a male reality, the experience male experience. And until the female side is acknowledged and recorded, the era cannot even begin to emerge in perspective.

Richard Schickel, in a recent essay entitled "Growing Up in the Forties," tries to elucidate the factors that shaped Middle-American adolescence. After discussing sports (baseball and football, activities from which the female sex was barred) as "Middle America's only universal metaphor," he goes on to describe with regret those painful scenes in the back seats of parked cars where sex was meted out piecemeal. "The curve of a breast briefly explored by two sly fingers making their way . . . through some interstice in a girl's clothing," runs his plaintive lament—"oh, God, was this to be all, forever?"

53

It is a lament endlessly repeated in most of the documents about those times. Gilbert Sorrentino's story "The Moon in Its Flight," Dan Wakefield's *Going All the Way*, Frederick Exley's *A Fan's Notes*, Philip Roth's *When She Was Good*, the screen's recent *Summer of '42*, *Carnal Knowledge*, and *The Last Picture Show*—however widely they may vary in tone, intent, subtlety, and success, all portray a monolithic male experience in which the War, movies, athletics, and the burden of sex denied emerge as the shaping forces of adolescent life, and girls, when presented at all, are the "problem."

The settings of my memories are frequently the same. Growing up in Ohio in the 1940s, I too was affected by those irresistible forces. Girls sat in the same movie theaters, attended the same football games, struggled in the back seats of the same parked cars. But the view from the bleachers is very different from the one on the field; and whether we gave in or held out in those parked cars, we had more fearsome concerns than simply making out. We were concerned with survival.

Our experience was no less important, our feelings no less urgent. Yet for some reason, only male versions have been recorded. Well, it certainly won't be the first time we were left out of the chronicles. Even back then it was the boys who delivered the graduation speeches; boys who got their pictures in the paper for football, win or lose; boys who, claiming the American privilege of free speech, spread slanderous things about us to boost their ratings. And the girls? The girls, when we were not simply ignored, were too often driven against our will to some dark lonely street where we were badgered or sweet-talked into going one step further than intended, and afterwards were frightened into silence. Only now are we beginning to speak.

WELL, THEN—WHAT WAS IT LIKE out there in a white middle-class suburban girl's Ohio in the cold decade between 1942 when I turned ten and 1952 when I turned twenty? What were we doing after school while the luckier boys were in varsity practice and the others were fielding high flies bounced off their garages? What were we feeling as we sat captive in our bedrooms waiting for our myriad pin curls to dry, the Hit Parade playing in the background? What forces, comparable in magnitude and significance to the War and Athletics, shaped our emerging consciousness and thus our destiny? What was it like among the bobby-soxers? In the bleachers? In the passenger seat of those borrowed cars in which boys drove us around and all too soon ruined everything by trying to feel us up?

In the early years of that decade we got together after school in each other's houses to talk about movie stars and play Monopoly, or to dress up in our mothers' clothes, jewelry, high heels, and lipstick, pretending we were seventeen going out on dates. If I couldn't ignore the sounds with which my brother filled up our house— his roar in the winter, his baseball games blasting on the radio in the summer—I tried to drown them out with my records of Frank Sinatra, over whom I "swooned"—my sexual initiation.

By the middle of the decade, wearing by then my own ruby lipstick, I got together with my friends in larger groups ("clubs," we called them in junior high, finding "sorority" too pretentious, though we gave our clubs Greek letter names), where we practiced for our futures by dancing among ourselves to the latest Big Band releases, leading and following by turns, and sometimes even practiced kissing.

After school I hung around the drugstore sipping nickel pop, or, sitting entranced in a listening booth of the local record store, tried to determine whose version of a recent hit was the best one out. I doodled certain initials on my notebooks, passed compromising notes in study hall, consulted a Ouija Board about chancy matters, whispered, knitted argyle sox in class for a constantly changing secret someone until the teacher made me stop.

In the evenings when my radio programs were over, my share of the dishes done, my homework finished, my hair set in pin curls for the night, I confided in each of my girl friends on the telephone until my parents exploded. When I was sure nothing more could happen that day, I spilled my surging feelings to my five-year lockup diary, the very form of which led directly into the future. And once in bed, I would not surrender to sleep until the last possible moment, but listened to the radio I kept beside my pillow, memorizing the lyrics of every love song, the inflections of every vocalist, and the arrangements of every instrumental. Living for music and love.

Some of us were happy in love, more of us were sad—but in either case we lived for the next climactic installment of our own true romance, be it a rumor, a look, a word, or an actual date. It might come unexpectedly in a corridor between classes, or by careful design on a weekend—at the Saturday afternoon picture show, at our occasional Saturday night pajama parties, or at our mixers following school basketball or football games. Even if we loved no boy at all, we might fake it or boost a friend's romance in order to have material on which to base a whole new week's conspiracy and something to enter in our tear-smeared diaries. In lean times, we dedicated songs on the radio, through the medium of snickering disc jockeys, to unsuspecting boys. ("Our songs," we called them, though we listened alone.)

On Friday nights, boys or no, we attended our club meetings wearing each other's borrowed sweaters over Peter-Pan-collared dickies and pleated-all-round skirts in specified combinations (pink and maroon, baby blue and royal, cherry and white for a start), shod in saddle shoes or penny loafers. Brands mattered. Some of us kept our bobby sox up with colorless nail polish; others, ignoring our mothers' warnings about cutting off our blood circulation, kept them up with rubber bands. Sitting on the floor in one another's living rooms (with our hair still in pin curls, to be combed out only moments before the meeting ended and the boys arrived), we planned "affairs"—hayrides, sleighrides, movie parties, turnabout dances—to which we might legitimately invite the boys. Glorious 1944 and 1948: the leap years of my youth.

Oh, those clothes! We tried them on for hours in department stores, we changed our outfits repeatedly before each date. In the only novel I have seen by a woman covering approximately that era, Patricia Dizenzo's *An American Girl*, some of the most evocative passages are those in which the narrator describes the clothes.

*If I had the money I would have bought a royal blue wool jumper . . .*
*a maroon skirt to wear with a white sweater, a black and white plaid*
*pleated wool skirt to wear with a long-sleeved red sweater, a black*
*watch-plaid skirt to wear with a white or navy sweater, a gray wool*
*straight skirt to wear with . . .*

And more, more. I remember Teddy Bear coats, the New Look, White Shoulders perfume, pointy Whirlpool bras (not infrequently improved with cotton stuffing), Ipana smiles, eyelash curlers. We had to sharpen our wits and reward our bodies with something, we who never knew the joy of football!

And can there really have been nothing more for us than clothes, dancing, music, boys?

Alas, there really was nothing more. Little else was permitted. Just as the boys practiced tackling and developed game plans to prepare them, as Schickel says, for "the wins and losses of life, especially the former," we prepared for the only thinkable future available to us: marriage. Even the vocational counselors who took over Heights High School two days per semester hinted that the kind of secretarial position we ought to apply for—legal stenographer, dental assistant, executive secretary—should be keyed, respectively, to the kind of husband we hoped to nab; unless we were so unimprovably plain that we needed some more permanent vocation to "fall back on"—in which case, if we were "college caliber," we were urged to train as teachers, librarians, nurses, or dieticians.

In my own brief, sheltered life I had already seen how far one could go as a secretary. Ever ambitious, I had gone from band secretary (handing out the music) to homeroom secretary (handing out homework) to nurse's aid (handing out hall passes) to running for the highest female office in the school: school secretary. When I lost, I ended my secretarial career.

We did sometimes go out for drama, for glee club, for art, for debating, piano, class politics, or even cheerleading (to this day I have yet to hear of a cheerleader scholarship to college); but the life they prepared us for was marriage, which was the sum of what, for most of us, life consisted. As in later years when men may have positions and families while women have only families, so in high school boys had football and love while we had only love. When we cheered, we cheered the boys: whatever hobby we cultivated, it too led ultimately down the aisle.

By the end of the decade we were openly and frankly discussing the subject with all its pitfalls and implications. What kind of husband did one want? What kind of wedding? How many children? How many bridesmaids? And trickiest of all—the part that gave us the heebie-jeebies—how in the world to snare one? For it was common knowledge that boys (who, with snowballs in winter and dunkings in summer, gave daily evidence of despising us) sought to avoid, or at least postpone, marriage as eagerly as we sought to achieve it. It was no secret. The entire culture conspired to show that life was a battle of the sexes: *them* against *us*. We knew, of course, that the boys would marry eventually: the question was, Could we get them to marry *us?* As Schickel observes, "It never occurred to us that there was some link between these [pinup] photos and the girls in school or the girls we passed in the streets," and that fact was readily apparent. How get them to notice us without ruining our chances by putting out? Wakefield succinctly captures the predominant male attitude toward marriage, at least as it was expressed by Middle American boys: "With the talk of marriage his prick had gone soft" (the very talk that held some promise of arousing us). Or, again: "Shit, he wouldn't get married. He was getting laid all over Chi." Such an attitude was simply impossible for a girl. In other places and other years a girl might manage to use sex to *get* a spouse (in *The Last Picture Show*, for example), but never, never to escape from one.

To snag a man. It was for that final, apocalyptic maneuver that I, like my sisters, wound up before the three-way mirror (as limiting as blinders and confining as a cage) practicing batting my eyes like Hedy Lamarr, flashing a smile like Betty Grable, wringing my hands like June Allyson, and night after night, equipped with comb, a glass of water for dipping, rubber-tipped bobby pins and metal clips, and a large triangular hairnet, setting my hair according to the instructions in every new issue of *Seventeen* magazine. As it was impossible for us to make our mark upon the world (except, eventually, through offspring), we had nowhere to make it but on ourselves. The mark to make and how to make it was all spelled out for us in every document of female adolescence: if our faces were round, we set our pin curls in one direction; if our jaws were square we set them in another. But no matter how we started out, if we studied the magazines and the movies and each other carefully enough, we could come up with the perfect formula for enhancing our assets.

Back in the early days, I confess, I wanted more. I remember pledging my daily allegiance to our 48-star flag with such ardor that my voice quavered and brought me ridicule. When the War started, I collected old newspapers and flattened tin cans with as much enthusiasm as my brother. And as a young teen-ager, I dreamed of getting a factory job—as much for the daring and glamour of it as for productivity and patriotism. But by that time my parents had only to convince me that, despite Veronica Lake and Rosie the Riveter, nice girls didn't work in factories (even though nice boys did) to induce me to abandon the ambition. Just as nice girls didn't wear too-tight skirts, or stockings to school, or their hair upswept.

In fact, the older we got, the longer grew the list of inviting things that nice girls didn't do. (*Nice Girl?*, with Deanna Durbin, was the first adult movie I ever saw. And though I didn't understand it at the time, I accepted the fact that the phrase "nice girl" would always be followed by a question mark.) Nice girls didn't smoke on the street. Nice girls didn't kiss on the first date. Nice girls didn't lead on the dance floor. Nice girls didn't curse (or allow cursing in their presence). Except to ask an opening question about sports, nice girls didn't take the initiative in conversation. Nice girls didn't show they were smart, speak out of turn, laugh at risqué jokes, hang around the football field or the pool hall, go unaccompanied to bowling alleys, dance halls, movies, beaches, skating rinks—anywhere, really, except to two or three specified restaurants. Nice girls didn't wear their heels the wrong height, their sweaters without slips, the wrong kind of bras, their hair the wrong style. Nice girls didn't talk to boys to whom they hadn't been introduced, clinch too long with boys to whom they had, and more important still, talk to girls who weren't nice girls.

With such a list of prohibitions—and plenty more coming up behind—who wouldn't want to light out like Huck and every other red-blooded American boy for the territories? Or at least go off on a weekend tear? But unfortunately, nice girls didn't do that either. Nice girls didn't even stay out after midnight unchaperoned.

And if we did? If, out of some adventurous spirit or sexual desire that managed to survive the poison of our puberty, we did break the rules—what happened then? We risked nothing less than our futures. A few lucky ones (I have met two or three), finding boys they could trust, actually managed to have good sex—a miracle, considering how dangerous a game they played. But for the rest of us, even the possibility of good sex disappeared before the specter of what we might be losing. For we risked losing the one asset that kept us listed on the Big Board in the Marriage Market—"respect"—and getting instead the one that scratched us off—a "reputation." And once that occurred, a girl turned from a nice girl, who at least had the right (as well as the duty) to protest a boy's sexual advances, into a "real girl," against whom anything went. According to conventional wisdom, ridicule was the least she deserved, but even rape, particularly if done in a gang, was forgivable. The hero of Exley's *A Fan's Notes* relates the circumstances of his sexual initiation:

*My initiation into sex had taken place on the ground behind a billboard sign advertising beer. . . . The girl had received, with neither complaint nor enthusiasm, a good part of Watertown High School's 1945 football team. Afterward I had had to help her up and walk her, while she clung unsteadily to my arm and wept, to her house some distance down the highway.*

In Wakefield's novel a slightly different sort of group spirit is shown to operate against the girl with a reputation:

*. . . whatever happened to Donna Mae Orlick [?]*
   *Big Quinn hooted and slapped his knee. "Married," he said. "Settled down. Can ya picture it?"*
   *"How'd it happen?" Gunner asked, in the tone of a man inquiring about a great pianist who had lost his fingers.*
   *"Some guy from Terre Haute knocked her up. She had a pie in the oven, and the guy married her."*
   *"Shit," Gunner said, "couldn't he have got three witnesses to testify?"*
   *It was said that if a girl got pregnant and you could get three other guys to testify they had fucked her, too, there was some law that said you didn't have to marry her because she was a loose woman or something. . . .*
   *"Buddy, you talk about* three—*he could of got three* hundred," *Big Quinn said. "But the guy was from* Terre Haute. *He didn't* know."

In Philip Roth's *When She Was Good*, the hero, Roy Bassctt, speculates about the possibilities of getting into a cheerleader, Ginger Donnelly:

*This fellow named Mufflin . . . said that his friends over in Winnisaw told him that at a party across the river one night, back in Ginger's freshman year . . . she had practically taken on the whole Winnisaw football team. The reason nobody knew about it was because the truth was immediately suppressed by the Catholic priest who threatened to have all those involved thrown in jail for rape if even one of them opened his mouth. It was a typical Mufflin story and yet some guys actually believed it—though Roy wasn't one.*

In fact, the image of the "real girl" who winds up "taking on the entire team" turns up again and again in male books about Middle America in that era. Whether she existed or not (and in either case, it was certainly not we who created her), she was always there in our consciousness, the terrible threat, the living alternative to being "good." No wonder, then, that my most intense memory of adolescence is that anxious moment in the back seat of the car (one scenario, many actors), although my lipstick has been smeared and my hair irreparably mussed, yet before my "please stop now" has been overruled, turning a promising intimacy into an anxious struggle.

IT WAS THE BOYS who put us in those compromising positions (we never asked to be driven to those dark streets), the boys who decided whether or not they would tell (we always begged them not to), the boys who imposed our dilemmas, knowing perfectly well what would happen to us if they went too far. Then why is it that men writing about the 1940s and 1950s so frequently misunderstand our concern with our reputations? Some of them, like Exley, find it mean and contemptible, some find it silly, dog-in-the-manger, or simply misguided. But few understand it as a survival response; few allow the legitimacy of our fears. To most of them it is simply the unfortunate source of their bad sex. Even in such a generally sympathetic story as Sorrentino's sensitive "The Moon in Its Flight," it is assumed that girls desired sex as much as boys, that it was only social circumstances or blind allegiance to a code that kept us apart.

But the fact is, for many of us who grew up in those days, once we understood the real consequences of indulging in sex, sex became a genuinely horrifying thing, not desirable at all. Even if it could have been practiced with finesse, which under the circumstances was hardly possible, who among us could have abandoned herself to it happily, knowing the consequences? When we said no, when we struggled to get the boys' hands off our breasts, when we crossed our legs in rigid rejection of those ubiquitous probing fingers, it was not because we were blindly, stupidly accepting some code handed down by our mothers. Our concern with virginity was not something we learned, as Schickel suggests, at the movies; not some gleeful conspiracy among us to deny boys their pleasure or some perverse way to titillate. It was hardly a matter of "pleasure" at all. The question of pregnancy quite aside, we early learned to ignore our reputations at our peril because of the sanctions that *they* imposed upon *us*—sanctions so damaging to our sexuality that many of us never managed to recover. Like the characters in the Feiffer-Nichols movie *Carnal Knowledge*, boys made it quite clear to us that there were certain kinds of girls they simply would not care to marry. In the cliché of the period, we had "nothing to gain and everything to lose" from submitting—as they had the very opposite. Nor was it a simple double standard we had to contend with; it was an inverse one, whereby, diabolically, we lost to the extent that they won, and vice versa. And worse: for if they lost, if they failed to "score" or even get, as they so blatantly analogized, to "first base," they were always free to try it again next inning. At best they wasted an evening's effort. But if one of us lost, we risked losing for good; once we gave in, we could never again expect our protests to be heeded.

Why did we cling to our reputations? As the fox who failed to catch the hare explained, "I was running for my dinner, but he was running for his life." Perhaps if we had been permitted access to some of life's touted rewards through other routes than sex and marriage; perhaps if the boys had been happy to marry us despite our reputations; perhaps if they had known how to keep their mouths shut or offered us reasonably good sex, we might then have been tempted to relent a little. But instead they offered us battle and frequently contempt. Not even nice girls were safe from it. "Where I had come from," says the narrator of *A Fan's Notes,*

> *seducing a "nice" girl was hard work. In the back seat of wintry cars one chewed on lower lips for longer periods of time than starlets cohabit with producers. One moved lower then, leaving a trail of perfumed saliva on ears and necks along the way, coming to plant already swollen lips on wool-sweatered nipples . . . meeting convulsive, furious hands all the way . . . Even if one did make it . . . one didn't dare look down in fear of seeing a half-dressed, broken-bra'ed bedraggled, pimply, snot-nosed, shivery-assed creature feigning her conscience-inducing sleep, trying not to moan.*

On balance, given the circumstances, I think we did well to fight them. When Betty Grable in some old movie of the 1940s whacked Don Ameche across the face for trying to kiss her, I think she probably had the appropriate impulse for the period.

IN A RECENT ISSUE OF *ESQUIRE* with a supplement on the 1940s and a Petty Girl swinging on the cover there is the statement: "The [1940s] were—well, *natural*, without pretense or guile."

Without pretense or guile? Boys among themselves, perhaps, where we could not overhear them (*Esquire* should know); in the locker room or the barracks maybe; but between boys and girls, as I recall, it was primarily pretense and guile. In fact, one reason we have such a hard time getting the story straight about those days is that evidently no one ever told the truth. About the thing that mattered most for us, our reputations, there were only lies. Whatever the boys did with the girls, they claimed to have done more; at the very least it was kiss and tell. ("It was really pretty much of a failure" says the narrator of *Going All the Way*, "if you parked with a girl and got only covered-tit and sometimes when Sonny just got covered-tit he actually lied if anyone asked and said he got bare-tit.") As for us, whatever we did or didn't do, we denied everything all the same.

Without pretense or guile? From *A Fan's Notes* again:

*If we were lucky . . . we ended in the sack with some long-legged, energetic, none-too-bright airline hostess who afterward wept while we assured her of our undying devotion, even as we plotted how to get rid of the creep.*

From *Going All the Way*:

*She thought Gunner's name was Ron. That was for safety, so if you ever knocked up one of those broads, they couldn't track you down. That's why Gunner introduced Sonny as "George."*

And even the young Catcher in the Rye, Holden Caulfield, Mr. Guileless-Charm himself, whose life was devoted to eschewing the "phony," whose dream spot was a cabin in the woods where "if anybody tried to do anything phony, they couldn't stay"—even Holden confesses to the usual equivocal back-seat-of-the-car hanky-panky:

*At first she didn't want to, because she had her lipstick on and all, but I was being seductive as hell and she didn't have any alternative . . . Just to show you how crazy I am, when we were coming out of this leg clinch, I told her I loved her and all. It was a lie, of course, but the thing is I meant it when I said it. I'm crazy. I swear to God I am.*

And maybe Roy Bassett meant it too in Philip Roth's spectacularly accurate parked-car scenes in *When She Was Good* (a book which, though widely hailed as the definitive portrait of the Great American Bitch, seems to recognize, even to understand, the Middle American girl's plight—and yet still manages to blame her for all the awful consequences):

> *There [at Passion Paradise] Roy would turn off the lights, flip on the radio, and try with all his might to get her to go all the way.*
> *"Roy, I want to leave now. Really."*
> *"Why?"*
> *"I want to go home, please."*
> *"I sort of love you, you know that."*
> *"Don't say that. You don't. . . ."*
> *In the back he told her how much he could love her. He was pulling at her uniform buttons.*
> *"Everybody says things like that when they want what you want, Roy. Stop. Please stop. I don't want to do this. Honestly. Please."*
> *"But it's the truth," he said, and his hand, which had touched down familiarly on her knee, went like a shot up her leg.*
> *"No, no—"*
> *"Yes!" he cried triumphantly. "Please!"*
> *"Roy—!"*
> *"But I love you. Actually now I do. . . ."*
> *"You say love," Lucy said. "But you don't mean love."*
> *"I get carried away, Lucy. That's not a lie. I get carried away, by the mood. I like music, so it affects me. So that's not a 'lie.' "*

Yes, even Richard Schickel, in whose innocence I believe and with whose longings I sympathize—even he will have to admit there was something less than guileless and certainly less than understanding going on in the parked cars where he and his friends hoped that "somehow in our pawings, pleadings and arguments we would stumble upon that magic combination of verbal and (shall we say?) subverbal appeals that would loosen the hold that virginity as a concept" had upon girls.

Most of the writers and directors who have been reconstructing the 1940s and 1950s for us have kept a certain distance from their period characters; they are clearly moved by something other than nostalgia. Those were not pretty times, and most of the writers who survived them seem to want to expose them. Feiffer's protagonists in *Carnal Knowledge* are shown to be the same sexual bullies as the boys I remember. The grim adolescent sex scenes in Bogdanovich's *The Last Picture Show*—hands rigidly clapped on thigh or breast without passion, much less tenderness, the very opposite of caresses—are remembered rightly with bitterness. Nevertheless, the girls are still presented neither with sympathy nor understanding. Somehow, when the stories are all over, when the callowness and conformity, elitism and racism of the time and place have been exposed and decried, the girls still come off looking like cock-teasers and ball-busters, or else, in the most cutting insult of the period, "beasts." In all those documents of the time of my youth, whether movie, essay, story, or novel, in those crucial battles in the back row of the movie house or on the floor in the living room or out behind the backstop or in the darkened back seat of a parked car—those scenes which are the very essence of pretense and guile—the girls somehow always wind up the culprits, bitchy or ridiculous, damned if they do and damned again if they don't.

It is that scene, with all its variations, that for me stands out as the paradigm of the era, as "Middle America's universal metaphor." Not sports (no, forgive me boys, not even football, without which, says Exley, life would have been inconceivable); not dancing, though at least that activity was open to both sexes and conformed in important respects to life's larger expectations (Holden Caulfield, the nicest sixteen-year-old boy in America, says: "Do you know when a girl's really a terrific dancer? . . . If I think there isn't anything underneath my hand—no can, no legs, no feet, no anything—then the girl's really a terrific dancer."); not yo-yoing, for which Frank Conroy in *Stop-Time* (as well as Abbie Hoffman in *Esquire*) makes such an inspired case. Not the Army, not the movies, not Captain Midnight or the Shadow. No. But if the Battle of Waterloo, as Wellington claims, was won on the playing fields of Eton; if the fate of Indochina, as Schickel suggests, was set on the scrimmage lines of Whittier, California; then the destiny of the female half of Middle America in times gone by was settled in the dirty back seat of some parked car as the male half relentlessly tried to score.

# ORGANS AND ORGASMS

THIS ESSAY IS NOT ABOUT lovemaking, a subject comprising emotional as well as anatomical considerations. Rather, it is about genital relations, and how they have adversely affected the lives of women. The myths and lies about female genital anatomy are so widespread and so harmful to women that the subject deserves an altogether separate consideration, even though it is only half the story.

Almost from the very beginning of our lives, we are all taught that the primary male sex organ is the penis and the primary female sex organ is the vagina. These organs are supposed to define the sexes, to be the difference between boys and girls. We are taught that the reason for the differences, and the use to which the sex organs are put, have to do with making babies.

This is a lie. In our society only occasionally are those organs used to make babies. Much more often they are used to produce sexual pleasure for men, pleasure which culminates in ejaculation. The penis and the vagina together can make either babies or male orgasms; very rarely do the two together make female orgasms. Men, who have benefited greatly from both orgasms and babies, have had no reason to question the traditional definition of penis and vagina as true genital counterparts.

Women, on the other hand, have. Woman's sexual pleasure

is often left out in these definitions. If people considered that the purpose of the female sex organs is to bring *pleasure to women*, then female sex would be defined by, and focused on, a different organ. Everyone would be taught from infancy that, as the primary male sex organ is the penis, so the primary female sex organ is the clitoris.

Men could never plead ignorance as they now commonly do, if from the beginning their sex education went something like this:

Boy: *What's the difference between boys and girls?*
Mother: *Mainly their sex organs. A boy has a penis and a girl has a clitoris.*
Boy: *What's a clitoris?*
Mother: *It's a tiny sensitive organ on a girl's body about where a penis is on a boy's body. It feels good to touch, like your penis.*
Boy: *Do girls pee through their clitorises?*
Mother: *No.*
Boy: *What's it for?*
Mother: *For making love, for pleasure. When people love each other, one of the ways they show it is by caressing one another's bodies, including their sex organs.*
Boy: *How do girls pee?*
Mother: *There's an opening below the clitoris for peeing. A man uses his penis for peeing, for making love, and for starting babies. Women have three separate places for these. For peeing they have an opening into the urethra; for making love they have a clitoris; and for the first step in making babies they have a separate opening into the vagina. A lot of other organs in women and men are used in making babies too.*
Boy: *How are babies made?* [And so on. . . .]

## Organs

IT HAS LONG BEEN KNOWN that the clitoris is endlessly more sensitive than the vagina, more sensitive than the penis too, if

70

one judges by the number of nerve endings in the organs. In fact, anatomically, the clitoris and the penis have many similarities since they develop from the same embryonic cells for the female or male fetus. Yet, as Ruth Hershberger pointed out in her brilliant 1948 book on female sexuality, *Adam's Rib*, society refuses to acknowledge it: "It was quite a feat of nature to grant the small clitoris the same number of nerves as the penis. It was an even more incredible feat that society should actually have convinced the possessors of this organ that it was sexually inferior to the penis."[1] The vagina, on the other hand, is for the most part so little sensitive that women commonly wear a diaphragm or tampon in it, and even undergo surgery on it, without feeling any sensation at all.

Despite the known anatomical facts and the experiences of many, many women, men usually insist that the vagina *is* the organ of female pleasure. Most of them insist, and probably believe, that women, like men, achieve orgasm by means of the movement of the penis back and forth into the vagina. While perpetuating this myth of vaginal primacy, from which they so readily benefit, the male "experts" make a small concession to the puzzling discrepancies in the facts. Taking their cue from Freud, they claim that there are *two* kinds of orgasm: vaginal and clitoral. But of the two, they argue, only the vaginal kind, which is adapted to the male anatomy and suits male pleasure, is necessary, is valuable; the clitoral kind is not.

Here is Freud himself:

*In the phallic phase of the girl, the clitoris is the dominant erotogenic zone. But it is not destined to remain so; with the change to femininity, the clitoris must give up to the vagina its sensitivity, and, with it, its importance, either wholly or in part. This is one of the two tasks which have to be performed in the course of the woman's development; the more fortunate man has only to continue at the time of his sexual maturity*

71

*what he has already practiced during the period of early sexual expansion.²*

A woman who fails to transfer her sexual sensitivity from the clitoris to the vagina at puberty is, according to Freud, regressive, infantile, neurotic, hysteric, and frigid. The vaginal orgasm is supposedly mature, beautiful, and good, while the clitoral orgasm is infantile, perverse, bad. A woman is frigid according to many of Freud's followers even today, if she does not have vaginal orgasms even though she may have frequent clitoral orgasms.

In their jokes and in their pornography, in their theories and in their marriage manuals, men treat the clitoris as simply one more erogenous zone like the breasts, underarms, or ears, to be used to arouse a woman sexually so that she will permit intercourse. They may remember the clitoris in foreplay, but for real sex, back to the vagina! The true center of female sexuality, the clitoris, is never identified for little girls who, when they accidentally discover they have one, often think themselves freaks to have on their bodies such a sensitive, unnamed thing. Most girls are not even told about the clitoris at puberty, when they may be instructed in the rites of feminine hygiene and intercourse. The diagrams of female genital anatomy that accompany most tampons and birth control devices usually illustrate the urinary bladder and the ovaries, but hardly ever the clitoris.

## Orgasms

WOMEN KNOW FROM PERSONAL EXPERIENCE that there is only one kind of orgasm, no matter what name it is given, vaginal, clitoral, psychological. It is a sexual orgasm. Women know there is only one set of responses, one group of things that happens in their bodies during orgasm. It may vary in intensity from one experience to another, but for any woman who has ever masturbated, orgasm is unmistakable and certainly cannot be confused with anything else. No woman masturbating ever wonders whether or not orgasm has occurred. She has no doubts about that. When it happens, she knows it.

The recent laboratory research on female sexuality conducted by Virginia E. Johnson and William H. Masters confirms clinically what women know to be true from their own experience. If a woman experiences orgasm during intercourse, it is not a special kind of orgasm with a special set of physiological responses; it is like any other orgasm. Without exception, the Masters-Johnson data show that all orgasms, no *matter what kind of stimulation produces them*, result in almost identical bodily changes for all women—vaginal contractions, increase in body temperature, increase in pulse and respiration rate, and so forth. Though it is produced through the clitoris, the orgasm occurs as well in the vagina, the anus, the heart, the lungs, the skin, the head.

Given this clarity about what an orgasm feels like, why then does a woman occasionally confess she "doesn't know" whether or not she has had orgasm during intercourse? If orgasm had occurred, she would know it. Since she does not know it, it cannot have occurred. Nevertheless, since she has been taught to expect some special kind of orgasm called vaginal orgasm which can occur only during intercourse, she wonders. She cannot know what such an orgasm is supposed to feel like because *there is no such thing.* The sensations of a penis in a vagina are indeed different from other sensations; accompanied by the right emotions they may be so pleasurable as to tempt a woman to hope that they can somehow qualify for that mysterious, desirable thing that has been touted as vaginal orgasm, even though they may not at all resemble the sensations she knows as orgasm. If she does not take advantage of the mystery and confusion surrounding the term to believe that perhaps she has indeed had a vaginal orgasm, she may feel compelled at least to pretend that she has. If not, she must submit to being called frigid or infantile by professional name-calling psychologists, doctors, and all who listen to them, and she must risk the displeasure and reprisal of her mate.

The truth is, there is only *one* kind of orgasm, one set of physiological responses constituting orgasm, all those Freudians to the contrary. The term "vaginal orgasm" must go. It signifies orgasm achieved by means of intercourse alone (for which no special term is necessary), or it signifies nothing at all. Some women testify to having experienced orgasm through intercourse alone; some women say they have experienced orgasm through stimulation of the breasts alone, or through stimulation of the mind alone, or during dreams. Apparently orgasm can be achieved by various routes. However, as the Masters-Johnson research shows, the most reliable way of regularly reaching orgasm for most women is by stimulation of the clitoris.

The clitoris may be stimulated to climax by a hand, by a tongue, or, particularly if the woman is free to move or to control the man's movements, by intercourse. No one way or combination of ways is "better" than any other, though women often prefer one way or another, finding that one way is rather more effective than another. Evidently for most women, intercourse by itself rarely results in orgasm, though vaginal stimulation may certainly make enjoyable foreplay or even afterplay. Masters and Johnson observe that the clitoris is automatically "stimulated" in intercourse since the hood covering the clitoris is pulled over the clitoris with each thrust of the penis in the vagina—much, I suppose, as a penis is automatically "stimulated" by a man's underwear whenever he takes a step. I wonder how often either is erotically stimulating by itself.

*Reactions*

THE WORD ABOUT THE clitoris has been out for a long time, and still, for political reasons, society goes on believing the old myths and enforcing a double standard of sexuality. Some societies have dealt with the facts by performing clitoridectomies—cutting off clitorises. More commonly, the facts about female sexuality are simply suppressed, ignored, or explained away. A century before Freud, for example, the learned Diderot cited woman's lack of control over her senses[3] to explain the infrequency of her orgasm during intercourse:

*There are some women who will die without ever having experienced the climax of sensual pleasures. . . . Since [women] have much less control over their senses than we, the rewards they receive from them are less certain and less prompt. Their expectations are being continually belied. With a physical structure so much the opposite of our own, the cue that sets their sensuality in play is so delicate and its source so far removed that we cannot be surprised at its not reaching fulfillment or becoming lost on the way.* [4]

Freud's ingenious formulation, though widely believed, is only one of many.

Since the Kinsey Report and the Masters-Johnson studies, it has become increasingly embarrassing to certain experts and self-styled lovers to go on ignoring the clinical facts and the testimony of women. In 1966 in an analysis of the Masters-Johnson research, Ruth and Edward Brecher listed three myths now recognized to have been disproved by the sex research, among them the myth that women have two kinds of orgasm, one clitoral, the other vaginal. The Brechers' conclusion was that "women concerned with their failure to reach 'vaginal orgasm' can thus be reassured."[5] But that is surely the wrong conclusion. It is not women who have been "failing" and must be "reassured." It is the male-dominated society that has been failing and must be changed. Many studies of female sexuality (95 percent of which, Masters and Johnson point out, are undertaken by men "either from the defensive point of view of personal masculine bias, or from a well-intentioned and often significant scientific position, but, because of cultural bias, without opportunity to obtain unprejudiced material")[6] remark on the spectacularly high degree of frigidity among women. Almost all of them interpret it as a failing of women, not of men or of society, despite the intrusive fact that, as Masters and Johnson observe, "women's . . . physiological capacity for sexual response infinitely surpasses that of man."

Although Masters and Johnson share the assumptions of our male culture that woman's goal must be to reach orgasm during intercourse—even though this usually requires getting to the brink of orgasm outside intercourse—in their newest report, *Human Sexual Inadequacy*, they examine the causes of "female sexual dysfunction" more honestly than their predecessors:

> *Sociocultural influence more often than not places woman in a position in which she must adapt, sublimate, inhibit, or even distort her natural capacity to function sexually in order to fulfill her genetically assigned role [i.e., breeding]. Herein lies a major source of woman's sexual dysfunction.*[7]

> *Probably hundreds of thousands of men never gain sufficient ejaculatory control to satisfy their wives sexually regardless of the duration of marriage or the frequency of natural sexual exposure.*[8]

> *Another salient feature in the human female's disadvantaged role in coital connection is the centuries-old concept that it is woman's duty to satisfy her sexual partner. When the age-old demand for accommodation during coital connection dominates any woman's responsivity, her own opportunities for orgasmic expression are lessened proportionately. . . . The heedless male driving for orgasm can carry along the woman already lost in high levels of sexual demand, but his chances of elevating to orgasm the woman who is trying to accommodate to the rhythm, depth, and power of his demanding pelvic thrusting are indeed poor.*[9]

> *The most unfortunate misconception our culture has assigned to sexual functioning is the assumption, by both men and women, that men by divine guidance and infallible instinct are able to discern exactly what a woman wants sexually and when she wants it.*

*Probably this fallacy has interfered with natural sexual interaction as much as any other single factor.*[10]

*The husband must not presume his wife's desire for a particular stimulative approach, nor must he introduce his own choice of stimuli.*[11]

But of the experts, Masters and Johnson are almost alone in not blaming women for the terrible betrayal of their sex lives.

Why? Clearly, this state of ignorance is not a result of simple unavailability of the facts. It is a manifestation of political and social choices. As Ann Koedt pointed out in "The Myth of the Vaginal Orgasm," "Today, with extensive knowledge of anatomy . . . there is no ignorance on the subject. There are, however, social reasons why this knowledge has not been popularized. We are living in a male society which has not sought change in women's role."[12] Now given our male-dominated society, the mere facts about female sexuality are not enough. The medical experts to this day find it easy to acknowledge the research evidence about the primacy of the clitoris—and *then* to dismiss its obvious meaning. Dr. Leslie H. Farber, for example, upon learning that the female orgasm is not produced by the vagina, simply throws out the importance of female orgasm. In a celebrated essay lamenting the Masters and Johnson research, Dr. Farber announced:

*As far as I know little attention was paid to female orgasm before the era of sexology. Where did the sexologists find it? Did they discover or invent it? Or both? . . . My guess, which is not subject to laboratory proof, is that the female orgasm was always an occasional, though not essential, part of woman's whole sexual experience. I also suspect that it appeared with regularity or predictability only during masturbation. . . . She was content with the mystery and variety of her difference from man, and in fact would not have had it otherwise.*[13]

But surely, some attention was paid to female orgasm before the era of sexology, or else how could it have appeared "with regularity . . . during masturbation"? What Dr. Farber apparently means to say is that before Kinsey little attention was paid to female orgasm *by men.* Too true. Why does Dr. Farber lament the findings of the sexologists? Because look what the findings do to a man's sex life. Nowadays, while ejaculating a man must "learn to take his moment in stride, so to speak, omitting the deference these moments usually call forth and then without breaking stride get to his self-appointed and often fatiguing task of tinkering with his mate—always hopeful that his ministrations will have the appearance of affection."[14] If a woman had to endure that attitude to reach orgasm outside of masturbation, no wonder she preferred to accept her "difference from man." As Masters and Johnson observe, "ejaculation . . . may provide welcome relief for the woman accepting and fulfilling a role as a sexual object."[15]

Donald W. Hastings, reviewing medical literature dealing with masturbation, observes a double standard of sexuality (and likely its cause) which in less sensational form persists to this day:

> *Articles in the older literature even went so far as to advocate the following procedures for correcting female masturbation: amputation or cautery of the clitoris,. . . . miniature chastity belts, sewing the vaginal lips together to put the clitoris out of reach, and even castration by surgical removal of the ovaries. [But, continues Dr. Hastings in a footnote,] there are no references in the medical literature to surgical removal of testicles or amputation of the penis to stop masturbation. One wonders what heroic measures might have been proposed for boys if women instead of men had composed the medical profession of the time.[16]*

Yes, one wonders. And one wonders what might have been defined as the major male and female sex organs, the standard sexual position, the psychic "tasks of development" as Freud called them, and, in fact, masculinity and femininity themselves, if women instead of men had composed not only the medical profession, but the dominant caste in society as well.

Men do not easily give up the myths about female sexuality because, whether they are aware of it or not, men benefit from believing them. Believing in the primacy of the vagina allows them to use women for their own sexual pleasure, while believing in vaginal orgasm frees them of responsibility for a woman's sexual pleasure: if a woman does not reach orgasm through intercourse, it is her own psychological failing. If they give pleasure to a woman another way, they are doing her a favor. It does not occur to them that, as Ann Koedt writes, "if certain sexual positions now defined as 'standard' are not mutually conducive to orgasm, they [must] no longer be defined as standard."[17] They do not admit that, as Ti-Grace Atkinson observes in "The Institution of Sexual Intercourse," "the whole point of vaginal orgasm is that it supports the view that vaginal penetration [by a penis] is a good in and for itself."[18] By perpetuating these myths society perpetuates the notion that women must be dependent solely on men for their sexual satisfaction and subordinate to the male interpretation of female pleasure.

## *The Discovery*

FOR THOUSANDS OF YEARS men have—perhaps unconsciously—benefited from these myths and have therefore believed them, nourishing them through all the various channels of culture, despite all the evidence to the contrary. But why have women, who know from experience that the vagina is not the source of their sexual pleasure, and who know only one kind of orgasm, believed in these myths?

Kept apart for so long, women until recently have been under great pressure not to discuss their sexual experiences with other women, just as Masters and Johnson were under great pressure not to study sex in the laboratory. Without information many women have, from childhood on, considered their own sexual experience exceptional and themselves inadequate, if not neurotic, infantile, frigid, or

ALIX KATES SHULMAN

simply freaks. Though each one recognized that the sex myths did not describe *her own* experience, she assumed that they did describe the experience of *other* women, about whom she had no real information. And many women secretly hoped that their own experience would some day follow suit. Now that women, the real experts on female sexuality, are beginning to talk together and compare notes, they are discovering that their experiences are remarkably similar and that they are not freaks. In the process of exposing the myths and lies, women are discovering that it is not they who have individual sex problems; it is society that has one great big political problem.

There are actually laws on the books in most states that define as "unnatural" and therefore criminal any (sexual) position other than that of the woman on the bottom and the man on the top; laws that make oral sex a crime though for many women it is the only way of achieving orgasm with another person; laws that make homosexuality a crime though for some people it is the only acceptable way of loving.

The pressures that have long made so many women forgo orgasm during love-making and fake orgasm during intercourse are real social pressures. The explanation that it is all simply a result of ignorance, men's and women's, will not do. Hopelessly isolated from each other in their cells in a male-dominated society, even with the facts around, women have still had to fake orgasm to keep their men, to hide their imagined or imputed inadequacy, to demonstrate "love," to gain a man's approval, to boost a man's ego, or, with orgasm nowhere in sight, to get the man please to stop. But with women getting together, the day may soon be approaching when they will exert enough counterpressure to define female sexuality in their own way, and to insist that, just as male sexuality is centered not in the scrotum but in the penis, female sexuality is centered not in the vagina but in the clitoris. When that happens, perhaps it will seem as perverse for a man to ejaculate without stimulating a woman to orgasm as it does now for a woman to reach climax outside intercourse.

Think clitoris.

## NOTES

1. Ruth Herschberger, *Adam's Rib* (New York: Pellegruni & Cudahy, 1948), p. 31.
2. Sigmund Freud, *New Introductory Lectures on Psycho-Analysis* (London: Hogarth Press, 1946), pp. 151–152.
3. It is not their senses, but their bodies over which women have less control than men: men control them.
4. Denis Diderot, "On Women" (1772), Lester Crocker ed., *Selected Writings*, tr. Derek Coltman (New York: Macmillan. 1966), p. 310.
5. Ruth and Edward Brecher, *An Analysis of Human Sexual Response* (New York: Signet, 1966), p. 84.
6. William H. Masters and Virginia E. Johnson, *Human Sexual Inadequacy* (Boston: Little, Brown. 1970), p. 214.
7. Ibid., p. 218
8. Ibid., p. 96.
9. Ibid., p. 229.
10. Ibid., p. 87.
11. Ibid., p. 301.
12. Ann Koedt, "The Myth of the Vaginal Orgasm," Shulamith Firestone and Ann Koedt, eds., *Notes from the Second Year: Women's Liberation* (New York, 1970), p. 39.
13. Leslie H. Farber, "I'm Sorry, Dear," Brecher and Brecher, *op. cit.*, p. 310. Emphasis added.
14. Ibid.
15. Masters and Johnson, *Human Sexual Inadequacy*, p. 93
16. Donald W. Hastings, "Can Specific Training Procedures Overcome Sexual Inadequacy?" Brecher and Brecher, *op. cit.*, p. 232.
17. Koedt, *op. cit.*, p. 38.
18. Ti-Grace Atkinson, "The Institution of Sexual Intercourse," Firestone and Koedt, *op. cit.*, p. 44.

# SEX AND POWER:
# SEXUAL BASES OF RADICAL FEMINISM

THIRTEEN YEARS HAVE PASSED SINCE a handful of radical feminists began organizing for women's liberation and analyzing every
aspect of the relations between the sexes, including the sexual. Not
that the subject of women's sexuality was ignored before then. Sex
had long been a "hot," salable subject. Men were studying it in labo-
ratories, in books, in bedrooms, in offices; after several repressive
decades, changes called the "sexual revolution" and "sexual liberation" were being widely discussed and promoted all through the
1960s; skirts were up, prudery was down. Nor was the sudden feminist attention to the political aspects of sexuality in the late 1960s
without precedent, as it appeared at the time; feminists have always
understood that institutions regulating relations between the sexes
were their concern.[1] But by the 1960s feminism itself had long been
in eclipse, and, far from being viewed as a political relation, sex
was considered a strictly biological, psychological, personal, or reli-
gious matter. Until the radical feminists boldly declared that "the
personal is political," opening for political analysis the most intimate aspects of male-female relations, women's sexuality had not

for decades been viewed squarely in its political dimension as an aspect of the power relations between the sexes.

In the nineteenth and early twentieth centuries, such sex-related institutions as family, motherhood, chastity, prostitution, birth control, and the double standard of morality had been subjected to feminist analysis by the "first wave" of feminists. Sexual repression had been privately acknowledged as a primary problem by the older Elizabeth Cady Stanton when she wrote in her confidential diary, begun at the age of sixty-five, "The first great work to be accomplished for woman is to revolutionize the dogma that sex is a crime."[2] But the suffragists and women's rights advocates mostly shied away from publicly discussing women's sexuality. Though first-wave feminists did focus on the connection between the subjugation of women and *male* sexuality[3], for the most part they did not make women's sexuality central to their analysis of woman's social condition, except as it affected other institutions, like motherhood.[4]

It was Simone de Beauvoir who reopened the subject of sex and power to feminist analysis in 1949 with the publication of *The Second Sex* in France. A year earlier, Ruth Herschberger, biologist and poet, had published the witty feminist analysis of female sexuality, *Adam's Rib*, in this country; but her ideas seemed too eccentric to postwar America to gain the audience they deserved.[5] A larger feminist context was needed—like that provided in Europe by Beauvoir's work and in this country by Betty Friedan's 1963 *The Feminine Mystique*, which signaled a second round of organized feminism.[6] In her book, Friedan discussed the use of sexual exploitation in advertising, the effect of sex roles on sexual fulfillment, and women's sexual discontents; but NOW, the organization Friedan founded to fight sex discrimination, did not at first concentrate on exposing injustice in the sexual sphere; indeed, that organization's early homophobia may even have exacerbated it. It remained for the radical wing of the new feminism—those mostly young women of the New Left whose discontent with their subordination by male radicals led them in the late 1960s to form the women's liberation movement (WLM to the FBI)—to make sexuality a central part of their analysis of sexism. Applying the analytic and organizational tools they learned in the civil rights movement and the New Left to their own situation, and drawing on the works of both Beauvoir and Friedan (as they would later draw on their earlier feminist predecessors), they used their sexual discontents to help them understand the power relations between men and women.[7]

By late 1967 small groups of women were meeting regularly to discuss the effects of male supremacy not only on women's professions, education, and public life, as the women in NOW were doing, but on their "private" lives as well. I was a fortunate participant. Those early discussions (which soon evolved into the technique called consciousness raising, later abbreviated CR) produced a great emotional outpouring of feelings against the way women had been used sexually and revelations of sexual shames and terrors we had all lugged through our lives. I was surprised to hear so many women who had come of age in the 1960s talk resentfully about their sexual experience, for I had believed the media version of the great sexual revolution among the young. But far from having felt freed by the so-called sexual revolution of the 1960s, those young, dedicated women—many of whom had been politicized in the New Left—actually felt victimized by it. They complained that they were expected not only to type the speeches, stuff the envelopes, and prepare the food and coffee for the radical men they worked with, but to sleep with them besides, without making any demands in return. Their own feelings, their needs for affection, recognition, consideration, or commitment, did not count. If they did not comply, they were often made to feel like unattractive, unhip prudes who could readily be replaced. Sexual favors were often the price of political favor. Naturally, these women resented being used sexually, as they resented performing political labors without appreciation, and resented being relegated to doing what they called movement "shitwork"—all by so-called radicals whose proclaimed purpose in life was to end oppression. And these women saw an intimate connection between the way men treated them in their organizations and the way they treated them sexually; they were two sides of a single demeaning attitude toward women— one that would not take them seriously.

As soon as the earliest radical feminist groups were organized many women without prior political experience began joining them and voicing other resentments. Some said they felt sexually rejected by their partners, others complained that their husbands never left them alone sexually. Some said they were afraid to tell their lovers what pleased them sexually, others said their partners resented being told. Some told about passes they had to submit to at work and on the street, others were bereft because men were intimidated by them and they, the women, were forbidden to make advances themselves. Some spoke about reprisals they feared or suffered as lesbians, others spoke of their fear of lesbians. Some shamefully confessed to having masturbated all their lives, others declared in anguish that they could not masturbate. Many complained bitterly that their men never took responsibility for birth control, for children, for the progress of their relationships.

The stories poured out. In those days, few of the women had had the opportunity to talk honestly about sex with anyone; it had been a taboo subject in the 1950s and was still suspect in the 1960s. Certainly, women had not felt free to talk about the intimate physical details; not only were sexual topics embarrassing, but sexual problems had long been taken as signs of personal failings or illness and as such were shameful, and talk about sexual secrets was considered a betrayal of your man and thus dangerous. I remember the excitement generated when the women in my group in 1967 first admitted to each other that they had been faking orgasm—and for various "reasons." Once the truth was out, we tried to analyze why so many of us had all felt the need to fake. Instead of feeling guilty about it, we saw faking as a response to pressures that had been put upon *us* by men.[8]

Still, no matter how liberating and exhilarating our discussions of such intimate matters may have felt our purpose was not simply to improve our sex lives or to find some personal solution to our problems. We wanted nothing less than to understand the social basis for our discontents, including the sexual, and then to do something to change it—for everyone.

This is a very important point. Consciousness raising was not simply a technique to make people feel better about themselves or to cure their personal problems. It was not therapy.[9] It was conceived as a political tool, modeled on the Chinese practice called Speaking Bitterness. The idea was this: The so-called experts on women had traditionally been men who, as part of the male-supremacist power structure, benefited from perpetuating certain ideas, and therefore what they said was suspect. If we were truly to understand the situation of women in out society, we had to base our analysis on information we could trust, information that was *not* suspect, and for this we had to gather it ourselves. We had to question all the generalizations that had been made in the past about women and question the interests they served, substituting knowledge based on the experience and feelings of women, starting with ourselves. Those early CR sessions were really fact-gathering sessions, research sessions on our feelings. We wanted to get at the truth about how women felt, how we viewed our lives, what was done to us, and how we functioned in the world. Not how we were *supposed* to feel but how we really did feel. This knowledge, gained through honest examination of our own personal experience, we would pool to help us figure out how to change the situation of women. Those early meetings felt like life-transforming discussions because our object was justice for all women.[10] We *had* to tell the truth; so much depended on it. We were going to change the world.

What made the discussions so powerful was the sense we had that a great floodlight had been turned onto the world, lighting up *all* our experience; it was as though all the murky and scary shadows we had been living with all our lives were suddenly wiped away by the powerful new light. Sex was a central and explosive subject to which we continually returned; but as we talked of our most intimate feelings we began to see how interconnected were all our experiences and our seemingly disparate lives.

Since everything we discussed was connected, we felt we could start anywhere in our analysis of women's lives: sex, class, work, marriage, motherhood, sex roles, housework, health, education, images, language—all these aspects of women's lives were riddled with sexism. The movement we envisioned would change them all.

A review of the major actions of those earliest years of WLM—actions initiated by a mere handful of ardent women, at first maybe 100 in 1967, then, by 1970, many thousands—reveals how central was the new feminist analysis of sexuality to our collective struggle for justice. In 1967 the first small groups began organizing and doing CR. By September 1968 the fledgling movement considered itself ready for its first national demonstration: about sixty feminists, mostly from New York, went to Atlantic City to picket the Miss America Pageant, using that event to demonstrate how women are (degradingly) judged as sex objects. Inside Convention Hall women unfurled a huge banner in the balcony that read, simply, Women's Liberation. Outside on the boardwalk, demonstrators mockingly crowned a live sheep "Miss America"; filled a "freedom trash can" with items of female "torture," like curlers, bras, girdles, and high-heeled shoes; spoke only to female reporters; and paraded with leaflets and posters. One of the most popular posters was a replica of a display ad for a popular steak house depicting woman's naked body charted with the names of beef cuts. The poster seemed a perfect symbol of the exploitation of women as sex objects, but the ideas of WLM were then so unthinkable that the demonstration was not well understood. Many onlookers and reporters were incensed; it was at that demonstration that feminists became known as "crazy bra burners," though no bra was burned. So acceptable was the practice of valuing women for their sexual attractiveness that many people genuinely believed the demonstrators must be ugly women, motivated by simple jealousy of the contestants, proclaiming a politics of sour grapes.

The following spring the newly formed Redstockings held their first abortion speak-out, at which women gave public testimony describing in heartrending detail what they had to go through to get abortions.

The testimony broke a very deep taboo and started a passionate public debate that is still going on. It is hard to believe how stunned the country was by this action. At the heart of the prohibition against abortion (and birth control) is the deeply held feeling that female sex outside of procreation must be punished. As a national columnist wrote at the time, "She had the fun, now let her pay." (In the same way, the early speak-outs on rape emphasized not only the brutality and hatred in the act of rape but the way in which, by society's "blaming the victim," women's sexuality was held responsible for rape—as reflected in laws, police procedures, and relevance of the victim's sexual history.) What was new at the abortion speak-out was that the women, speaking of their feelings and experience and pain, tied abortion to the question of women's freedom, which had not been done publicly since the birth control debates of an earlier time. Indeed, what prompted the Redstockings speak-out was a legislative hearing on abortion at which the "experts" testifying were fourteen men and one woman, a nun. The Redstockings thought it time to hear from the "real experts": women.

Those earliest years witnessed a proliferation of actions, from a Whistle-In on Wall Street, in which feminists made sexual passes at men on the street at lunchtime, to a protest at the National Bridal Fair by WITCH (Women's International Terrorist Conspiracy from Hell), to a takeover by New York Radical Feminists of legislative hearings on prostitution—all intended to raise public consciousness of sexism. The insults flung at demonstrators by angry observers at these demonstrations were predominantly sexual: we were called dykes, whores, and beasts, as well as commies, bitches, and nuts.

In 1969 a coalition of feminist groups staged a sit-in at the *Ladies Home Journal* offices until we were granted twenty pages in which to present feminist ideas to the *Journal*'s vast female audience. I joined the committee that wrote the article on sex. Many of the articles the *Journal* editors could stomach, but the sex piece scandalized them—in part because it briefly discussed lesbianism, but also, I think, because it so clearly brought together the private and public, the personal and political. Late in 1969 the historic First Congress to Unite Women was held in New York City, attended by more than 500 women. That same year, 1969, Barbara Seaman's *The Doctor's Case against the Pill* was published. Then, in 1970, came Kate Millett's *Sexual Politics*, Shulamith Firestone's *Dialectic of Sex*, and the first of the large publishers' anthologies of articles and pamphlets that had been circulated earlier in movement journals: Robin Morgan's *Sisterhood Is Powerful*, Leslie Tanner's *Voices from Women's Liberation*, Sookie Stambler's *Women's Liberation: A Blueprint for the Future*, and, the next year, Vivian Gornick and B. K. Moran's *Woman in Sexist Society*, and others—all including important articles on sexuality. There was a great outpouring of articles, stories, books, conferences, demonstrations, debates. Lesbian feminists began forming separate groups and exploring the connections between lesbianism and feminism; at the Second Congress to Unite Women (1970), a radical lesbian group calling themselves the Lavender Menace forced the movement to examine its attitude toward lesbianism. The women's self-help movement encouraged women to examine their own and each other's bodies, inside and out, not only to overcome ignorance and shame, but to free us from the bias and control of the male medical establishment. New York Radical Feminists and other groups outside New York organized speak-outs, frequently modeled after those early Redstockings abortion speak-outs, on such volatile topics as rape, prostitution, marriage, motherhood. Feminist ideas were spreading everywhere as we made new connections and more women joined the movement. It seemed to us then that we could not be stopped.

# 2

WHAT WERE THE EARLY RADICAL feminist ideas about sex? Naturally, as WLM was a political movement the new attention directed by radical feminists to women's sexuality had to do with power; with taking for ourselves the control of our lives and our bodies that men—through laws, customs, and other institutions of a male-ruled society—had appropriated. The feminist movement for reproductive freedom, the women's self-help movement from California, the broader women's health movement—of which the Boston collective's best-selling *Our Bodies, Ourselves* was a product and a source—all organized around the idea of reclaiming for ourselves control over our very bodies. So with the new feminist analysis of sexuality.[12] Perceiving sexual relations as but one aspect of the power relations between men and women, early radical feminists questioned traditional definitions of women's sexuality, of women's "nature," of sexual satisfaction and health (conceived as heterosexual) on the grounds that such definitions, as propounded by men, tended to justify the sexual exploitation of women by men. "If sexual relations were not programmed to support political ends—that is, male oppression of the female—then the way would be clear for individuals to enter into physical relations not defined by roles, nor involving exploitation. Physical relations (heterosexual and homosexual) would be an extension of communication between individuals and would not necessarily have a genital emphasis," read a 1969 position paper put out by "The Feminists: A Political Organization to Annihilate Sex Roles."[13]

"We must begin to demand that if certain sexual positions now defined as 'standard' are not mutually conducive to orgasm, they no longer be defined as standard. New techniques must be used or devised which transform this particular aspect of our current sexual exploitation,"[14] proclaimed Anne Koedt in her famous essay, "The Myth of the Vaginal Orgasm," published in 1968 in *Notes from the First Year* and expanded the following year. Though Koedt focused on technique, the point of her article was clearly political. She was concerned not only with the true facts about female orgasm, then under scrutiny by sexologists, but with exposing the distortion of those facts into the "myth" of the vaginal orgasm:

*Today, with extensive knowledge of anatomy . . . there is no ignorance on the subject [of female orgasm]. There are, however, social reasons why this knowledge has not been popularized. We are living in a male society which has not sought change in women's role. . . .*

*The establishment of clitoral orgasm as fact would threaten the heterosexual institution. For it would indicate that sexual pleasure was obtainable from either men or women, thus making hetero-sexuality not an absolute, but an option. It would thus open up the whole questions of human sexual relationships beyond the con-fines of the present male-female role system.*[15]

This analysis was continued by Ti-Grace Atkinson, a founder of The Feminists, the early antimarriage group which limited to one-third of its membership those women who lived with men. In "The Institution of Sexual Intercourse," in *Notes from the Second Year*, Atkinson analyzed sexual intercourse itself as a "political institution," analogous to the institution of marriage, which serves the needs of reproduction and often the sexual desires of men but not necessarily those of women. Atkinson coolly proposed that we try to "discover what the nature of the human sensual characteristics are from the point of view of the good of each individual instead of what we have now, which is a sort of psychological draft system of our sexualities." Never reducing sexual relations to mere technique, Atkinson elaborated the insight that orgasm is not everything by observing that what lovers add to the sexual experience "cannot be a technique or physical improvement on that same auto-experience" but "must be a psychological component."[16]

Carrying the feminist rebellion against the sexual exploitation of women a step further still, Dana Densmore of Boston's Cell 16 proposed a reordering of women's priorities away from the sexual altogether. After all, the belief that sexual love of man is the core of woman's aspirations—or is even necessary for fulfillment—jus-tifies woman's exploitation and keeps her enthralled. In her pow-erful 1969 essay, "On Celibacy," which appeared in the first issue of *No More Fun and Games*, the journal associated with Cell 16, Densmore wrote:

> *We must come to realize that we don't need sex, that celibacy*
> *. . . could be desirable, in many cases preferable to sex. How*
> *repugnant it is, after all, to make love to a man who despises*
> *you, who fears you and wants to hold you down! Doesn't screw-*
> *ing in an atmosphere devoid of respect get pretty grim? Why*
> *bother? You don't need it. . . . This is a call not for celibacy*
> *but for an acceptance of celibacy as an honorable alternative,*
> *one preferable to the degradation of most male-female relation-*
> *ships. . . . Unless you accept the idea that you don't need [men],*
> *don't need sex from them, it will be utterly impossible for you*
> *to carry through, it will be absolutely necessary for you to lead*
> *a double life, pretending with men to be something other than*
> *what you know you are. . . . If we are going to be liberated we*
> *must reject the false image that makes men love us, and this*
> *will make men cease to love us. . . . An end to this constant*
> *remaking of ourselves according to what the male ego demands!*
> *Let us be ourselves and good riddance to those who are then*
> *repulsed by us!*[17]

Writing on "Lesbianism and the Women's Liberation Move-ment," Martha Shelly, an early Radicalesbian, pursued Densmore's argument down another path:

> *To me, lesbianism is not an oddity of a few women to be hid-*
> *den in the background of the Movement. In a way, it is the heart*
> *of the Women's Liberation Movement. In order to throw off the*
> *oppression of the male caste, women must unite—we must learn*
> *to love ourselves and each other, we must grow strong and inde-*
> *pendent of men so that we can deal with them from a position*
> *of strength. The idea that women must teach men how to love,*
> *that we must not become manhaters is, at this point in history,*

*like preaching pacifism to the Vietcong. Women are . . . told to be weak, dependent and loving. That kind of love is masochism. Love can only exist between equals, not between the oppressed and the oppressor.*[18]

Thus, the price of maintaining sexual relations with men in a sexist society sometimes seemed too high to pay for many radical feminists, just as the price of motherhood in a sexist society has made many women reasonably decide to forgo that experience as well. But most radical feminists, rather than renounce heterosexuality, advocated struggle to change its basis. (Many considered separatism a cop-out.) In *The Dialectic of Sex*, Shulamith Firestone, shrewdly analyzing prevailing heterosexual relations, tried to specify the price women pay for male love. In the chapter on "Love," she describes love as requiring "mutual vulnerability or it turns destructive: the destructive effects of love occur only in a context of inequality." But because men and women are not equal, love is destructive for women. While "a man must idealize one woman over the rest in order to justify his descent to a lower caste,"[19] it is different for women:

*In their precarious political situation, women cannot afford the luxury of spontaneous love. It is much too dangerous. The love and approval of men is all-important. To love thoughtlessly, before one has ensured return commitment, would endanger that approval. . . . In a male-run society that defines women as an inferior and parasitical class, a woman who does not achieve male approval in some form is doomed. . . . But because the woman is rarely allowed to realize herself through activity in the larger (male) society—and when she is, she is seldom granted the recognition she deserves—it becomes easier to try for the recognition of one man than of many; and in fact this is exactly the choice most women make. Thus once more the phenomenon of love, good in itself, is corrupted by its class context:*

*women must have love not only for healthy reasons but actually to validate their existence.*[20]

To this end, women must subordinate their true feelings, cultivate sex appeal, aspire to meet beauty standards, inhibit sexual spontaneity, and even fake orgasms—anything to catch a man. It is less this behavior many radical feminists deplored than the condition of unequal power and vulnerability between the sexes that makes such behavior seem necessary for survival. As Jennifer Gardner wrote in the essay "False Consciousness" that was published in the California journal *Tooth and Nail*, "Our oppression is not in our heads. We will not become unoppressed by 'acting unoppressed.' Try it—if you have the economic independence to survive the consequences. The result will not be respect and support. Men will either not like you—you are a bitch, a castrator, a nag, a hag, a witch; or they will accuse you of not liking them."[21] As Kathie Sarachild wrote, observing the double nature of sex and power, "For most of history sex was, in fact, both our undoing and our only possible weapon of self-defense and self-assertion (aggression)."[22]

That some women seem to be able to have satisfactory sexual relations with men is as much beside the point, given sexism, as that some manage to gain economic security: sexual (and economic) injustices nevertheless prevail. From the point of view of radical feminism, which addresses the problems of the many, not of the privileged few, even the best "individual solutions" will be chancy, for unless a woman is strong and independent her solution can disintegrate when she alienates her male protector, which happens to many women simply by aging. (The early feminist group OWL, Older Women's Liberation, defined "older" as thirty and up—by prevailing sexist standards a ridiculous cut-off age for men but a realistic one for women considered as sex objects.) Irene Peslikis placed at the head of her list of "Resistances to Consciousness": "Thinking that our man is the exception and, therefore, we are the exceptions among women. . . . Thinking that individual solutions are possible, that we don't need solidarity and a revolution for our liberation."[23] As for those "personal solutions" which do not depend on male protection but involve withdrawal from men, women who choose them are subject to all the sanctions, reprisals, and punishments traditionally dealt to women without men under male supremacy. "Until we have a movement strong enough to force change," wrote Firestone in *Notes from the Second Year*, "we will have to accommodate ourselves as best we can to whichever . . . adjustment each of us can best live with," never forgetting, however, as Anne Koedt wrote in *Notes from the First Year*, "to go to the root of the problem rather than become engaged in solving secondary problems arising *out* of [woman's] condition." Just as women without control over reproduction will feel sexual anxiety, so women without control over conditions for their survival will also suffer sexual anxiety. From the beginning, radical feminists had differing analyses of sexuality, but all agreed that sexual relations were deeply affected by the general power relations prevailing between the sexes, that the way to change sexual relations was through solidarity and struggle to change power relations, and that the way to discover how these relations oppressed women was through consciousness raising.

# 3

FEMINIST IDEAS WERE SPREADING SO fast that it seemed to many of us in those days that it would not be difficult to organize masses of women to revolt. (Firestone thought it would take "several more years" to build a strong enough movement to "force change.") When the first mass August 26 Woman's March was held in large cities all over the country in 1970 to commemorate the fiftieth anniversary of the women's suffrage amendment and to demonstrate our power—as thousands of women marched to demand their rights—it looked as if we might win with ease. And in the years immediately following, our hopes rose as the ERA passed through Congress for the first time since its introduction fifty years before; as the Supreme Court ruled that abortion, at least in the first trimester, was a woman's right; as suits for equal pay were launched against large corporations; as prestigious all-male colleges, professions, and institutions considered admitting women.

However, even then a powerful resistance was organizing. After a few years had passed, almost everything remained to be done. People spoke differently but acted pretty much as they always had. Following our initial success came a certain foreboding. Alice Paul, the veteran suffragist who had witnessed the defeat of feminism once, warned against allowing a time limit to be attached to the ERA; but, heedless of history as Americans—especially the young—tend to be, too ready to project our own changed consciousness onto the world, feminists failed to heed her. In time it became clear that our expectations were too optimistic; we had changed only the surface of what was wrong. Even if every woman acknowledged the injustice of sexism and every man acknowledged the role of the clitoris in female orgasm, sexual strife would continue, because the sexual arrangements of the world were still based on unequal power. Organized antifeminism followed each of the movement's successes in changing public consciousness. Movement or no movement, feminist feelings were not given public expression, our testimony was not considered "expert," our power in the world of public decisions remained miniscule. The heart of our sexual dissatisfaction with men was still that without power women were forced to sell it or forgo it, and we were still powerless. Even if we objected to Miss America standards we still had to be judged by them in our daily lives and then be tossed on the junk heap when we no longer measured up. Reexamining everything, even achieving *perfect understanding*, was not going to be enough to enable us to change the relations between the sexes, because sex had to do with power and those with power were not about to smile sweetly and give it up. A long, difficult struggle would have to follow understanding.

This is not to discount the considerable political gains we did make during the 1970s in the fight for sexual justice. Of all the movements that emerged in the 1960s, the WLM was the one that most securely became a mass movement. Out of those early efforts grew changed attitudes and laws regarding women's work, reproductive freedom, physical abuse, and vast changes in notions of family. But many of the changes are extremely vulnerable to the growing anti-feminist backlash, and if we stop far short of our original goals we may lose the gains we have won. It happened to the women in the first wave— they gained certain important but only partial victories, and they were defeated and silenced for decades. It could happen to us if we let up the pressure or lose sight of our original goals. If consciousness can be changed once, twice, it can be changed again. We are experiencing a strong move to the right. Sterilization abuse, hormone abuse are on the *rise*. The gap between average male and female income is *larger* than it was a decade ago. If abortions were outlawed again, if women were pushed back out of the work force, if we returned to viewing sex as an exclusively private matter affecting each person in isolation rather than a political matter affecting all of us, it could happen again. Just as frightening as the organized political backlash, which at least we know how to fight, is the backsliding of consciousness, the erosion of radical feminist ideals. The radical feminist critiques of sexuality and sexual repression, originally presented as aspects of a much larger male domination of women but hardly as leading by themselves to solutions, have been diverted into concern with mere sexual technique or increased activity. Co-optation and tokenism have made it easier for people to deny that anything is still drastically wrong between the sexes. Again and again it is claimed that women have won sexual equality because the family is in a state of flux and chaos; that since the pill there is no longer any double standard—as if fear of pregnancy (which persists in any case) were the sole source of women's sexual anxiety. People say we are equal because a relatively small number of women are in positions of token power. (As with all "individual solutions," token power is different from real power, because as soon as the women who have it refuse to play the game they will lose their positions; knowing this, they are mostly supporters of the men to whom they owe their power.) But these facts only disguise the persistence of women's relative powerlessness.

A new generation does not know that ten years ago what are now our basic demands were unspoken, many even unmentionable. The ideas of women's liberation that were so recently shocking, thrilling, and liberating are already put down by many of the young as old hat and boring and by the old as a fad that is passé, obliterated in the swing of the pendulum. The presentation of feminism in the mass media has trivialized the movement's goals; in the name of "liberation" courses for women too frequently teach self-promotion instead of understanding and changing sexism in society; books on sexuality too often focus on technique and, worse, on how women may make themselves more sexually appealing to men, teaching us to blame the victim rather than on how to end victimization. The renewed search for personal solutions to collective problems is as arid today as it was a decade ago. Personal solutions to sexual problems center on finding the right partner or the right attitude or the right technique—at best chancy, at worst harmful, since they obscure the power relations inherent in sexual relations.

Several years back some of the women from the earliest movement days got together to discuss the changes that had occurred in their own sex lives since the movement began. All agreed that sex had changed for them, but very few thought it had really improved. True, some of them were now able to specify what they wanted their sex partners to do, but in some relationships the man resented the woman's desires. Several women who had changed from nonorgasmic to regularly orgasmic were sorry to find that nevertheless they were unhappy in love. Some of the women who had come out as lesbians found themselves facing a whole new set of problems and anxieties in a world that punishes homosexuality.[24] One woman grieved that since she no longer "played the game" she was no longer interested in sex at all and another that no one wanted her.

Not even the most ardent feminist can claim to be "liberated" in a sexist society. "Sexual liberation" can mean nothing unless it includes the freedom to reject or enter into sexual relationships fearing neither exploitation nor punishment. But sexual exploitation and punishment still threaten every woman. The denial of complete reproductive freedom, the total responsibility for child rearing, the psychological intimidation of rape victims are all punishments for the sexually active woman. The threat of job loss, ridicule, rejection, isolation, and even rape are punishments threatening the woman who refuses sex.

As radical feminist ideas are absorbed by institutions adept at deflecting change through co-optation, and as our radical programs come under direct attack by an increasingly vocal conservative backlash, our awareness of the political dimension of sexual relations, with its powerful potential for change, is in danger of being lost. Conceiving sexual liberation apart from feminist liberation can land us where women have too often landed—not with more real freedom but with new pressures to put out or to withhold. Our only recourse is to deepen our radical insights about the connections between sex and power and build a political movement which can put insight into action.

## NOTES

1. Linda Gordon traces the development of feminist ideas about sexuality in the United States, especially as they pertain to birth control, in *Woman's Body, Woman's Right: A Social History of Birth Control in America* (New York: Penguin Books, 1977).

2 Miriam Schneir, ed., *Feminism: The Essential Historical Writings* (New York: Random House, 1972), p. 145.

3. In her chapter "Social Purity," Linda Gordon writes that "feminists believed that men had developed excessive sexual drives which contributed to the subjection of women and hence limited the development of the whole civilization. From this they drew the inference that excessive sex drive had to be *eliminated*, not merely checked or sublimated, in order to create a pure and sexually equal society" (pp. 118–19).

4. Outstanding among exceptions were the free-love advocates, notably the

notorious Claflin sisters, Victoria Woodhull and Tennessee Claflin, who wrote frequently on the connection between sexuality and oppression in their publication of the 1870s, *Woodhull and Claflin's Weekly*. Dora Marsdon is quoted by Elaine Showalter in *A Literature of Their Own* (Princeton, N.J.: Princeton University Press, 1977) as proposing in 1913 that frigidity is the result of repression and economic dependence. The anarchist Emma Goldman spoke on injury to woman's sexuality resulting from male domination and publicly defended homosexual rights. See *Red Emma Speaks*, ed. Alix Kates Shulman (New York: Random House, 1972).

5. Ruth Herschberger, *Adam's Rib* (New York: Peligrini & Cudahy, 1948).

6. Betty Friedan, *The Feminine Mystique* (New York: Norton, 1963).

7. Sara Evans recounts the emergence of radical feminism from the civil rights movement and the New Left in *Personal Politics: The Roots of Women's Liberation in the Civil Rights Movement and the New Left* (New York: Alfred A. Knopf. Inc., 1979). Although Evans does not discuss radical feminist analyses of sexuality, she does document the sexual insults and exploitation of women within the New Left and the persistent refusal of the male radicals to take the complaints of the women seriously. For a firsthand account of the sexual resentments of New Left women, see Marge Piercy's essay "The Grand Coolie Damn," in *Sisterhood Is Powerful*, ed. Robin Morgan (New York: Random House, 1970).

8. This attitude is explored in the article, "When Women Rap about Sex," evidently the transcript of a meeting edited by Shulamith Firestone, in one of the first publications of the women's liberation movement, *Notes from the First Year* (New York: New York Radical Women, 1968).

9. In "The Personal Is Political," an article by Carole Hanisch in *Notes from the Second Year: Women's Liberation, Major Writings of the Radical Feminists*, ed. Shulamith Firestone (New York: New York Radical Feminists, 1970), Hanisch discusses the differences between therapy and CR groups.

10. In her widely disseminated "A Program for Feminist Consciousness Raising," in *Notes From the Second Year*, Kathie Sarachild, a founding member of Redstockings and theoretician of consciousness raising, repeatedly emphasizes the importance of connecting personal testimony with testimony of other women, now and in the past, and with political organizing.

11. The other source of the abortion movement was the population-control

movement, which in some ways promotes the opposite of women's freedom. For the relation between the feminist and population-control movements as they apply to birth control, see Gordon.

12. Pre-WLM feminist analyses of female sexuality include Herschberger's *Adam's Rib* (see n. 5 above) and Mary Jane Sherfey's 1966 paper for the *Journal of the American Psychoanalytic Association*, "The Evolution and Nature of Female Sexuality," based on her studies of multiple orgasm in women. After WLM was launched, *Adam's Rib* was reissued in paperback by Harper and Row, and Sherfey's essay was published in *Sisterhood Is Powerful* as "A Theory of Female Sexuality" and later expanded into a book.

13. *Notes from the Second Year,* p. 114.

14. Anne Koedt, "The Myth of the Vaginal Orgasm," reprinted in *Voices from Women's Liberation,* ed. Leslie Tanner (New York: New American Library/ Mentor Books, 1970), p. 159.

15. Ibid., pp. 161 and 166.

16. Ti-Grace Atkinson, "The Institution of Sexual Intercourse," in *Notes from the Second Year,* pp. 45–46.

17. Tanner, pp. 264–68.

18. Martha Shelly, "Lesbianism and the Women's Liberation Movement," in *Women's Liberation: a Blueprint for the Future,* ed. Sookie Stambler (New York: Ace Books, 1970), p. 127.

19. Shulamith Firestone, *The Dialectic of Sex: The Case for Feminist Revolution* (New York: Bantam Books, 1970), pp. 130–31.

20. Ibid., p. 138.

21. Jennifer Gardner, "False Consciousness," reprinted in *Notes from the Second Year,* p. 82.

22. Sarachild, p. 78.

23. Morgan, p. 337.

24. Sydney Abbott and Barbara Love observe that lesbians "suffer the oppression of all women but are not eligible for any of the rewards. . . . Fear of punishment creates tremendous anxiety, even though punishment may not occur" ("Is Women's Liberation a Lesbian Plot?" in Gornick and Moran, pp. 443 and 445).

# WRITING

# THE TAINT

"YUCK!" SAID MY FRIEND WHEN I asked her to tell me her reaction to feminist fiction.

I stare at her. Is she being provocative or sincere? A feminist activist and journalist who has no problem with either feminism or fiction, who claims she eagerly gobbles up feminist nonfiction as it rolls from the presses and is in fact writing her own book of it, my friend now goes even further, admitting she would probably avoid a novel presented to her as feminist. When she chooses fiction, she declares, she tries to select novels known to be delicious, moving, wonderful—and forget the politics—although naturally she would consider it a bonus if a good novel turned out to be feminist, too.

I'm shocked. Some of the most delicious, moving, and, yes, wonderful fiction I know seems to me patently feminist, from *Jane Eyre* to *The Golden Notebook* to *The Woman Warrior* (thinking only of novels written in English). What can be going on if even a self-proclaimed feminist like this friend has a prejudice against feminist fiction? What of the rest of the world? Am I—a veteran of the women's movement who has been writing fiction for more than two decades, including one novel about the rise of the contemporary women's movement—am I so out of touch that my friends must go out of their way to tell me?

Like every writer, I hope to be read sympathetically. Maybe I need to slow down and rethink this label before brazenly parading around in it in print. I feel fairly comfortable as a feminist and as a novelist; but as a feminist novelist? What's in a name? What is feminist fiction anyway? And who sez?

My first two novels were knocked or praised as feminist novels, but my second two, which personally seem to me equally feminist from the point of view of themes, controlling vision, audience, aim, author's politics, or any other approach I can think of, were each praised or knocked for *not* being so. For example, the late Anatole Broyard—no friend to feminism, fictional or otherwise—began his *New York Times* review of my third novel with: "After two rather trendy [read: feminist] novels, Alix Kates Shulman has written a selfless, careful, and satisfying book [read: not-feminist]." Maybe a step up from being judged by my gender, but possibly only a side-step. I'm confused.

As someone practiced in examining intellectual and political issues in company with her women friends, I decided to ask a few more people what they think about feminist fiction. Those I consulted include not only fellow fiction writers but also a few critics, an editor, a scientist, journalists, several academic feminists—all writers and word-people who, I figured, would be savvy about the meanings and implications of at least the key terms. In their own work these women write perceptively about women. All are deeply engaged in reading, teaching, writing about, and encouraging women writers, rescuing forgotten women writers of the past from oblivion, and generally countering the entrenched, exclusionary, white male literary elite guard. How surprised I was to find them as hesitant as I in the face of my questions—some enthusiastic, but some suspicious, confused, wary, defensive, or even hostile. The very idea of feminist fiction is surprisingly charged.

Eventually, everyone calmed down and turned thoughtful.

What is feminist fiction? Spiraling downward from the broadest to the narrowest descriptions, my friends' tentative answers included fiction that: demonstrates the authenticity of women's experience, centers on what it is to be a woman in culture, dramatizes the constraints on women under patriarchy, examines patriarchal institutions, is self-conscious about gender and traditional gender arrangements, challenges patriarchal modes of writing, portrays strong, independent women, embodies feminist attitudes, explores feminist themes, centers on feminist characters, aims to advance feminist causes, or is written by a feminist.

Whew! It seems that feminist fiction can be either an oceanic category, large enough to encompass a good part of the totality of women's fiction, or a deep puddle, including only a handful of works by a select group of self-proclaimed feminist writers whose works are saturated with feminist consciousness or portray feminist life—as, say, gay fiction reflects gay consciousness and portrays gay life.

Is this because the winds of deconstruction have left all general categories and identities notoriously shaken? When such formerly seaworthy terms as *woman, feminist,* and *fiction* are wobbling like rowboats in a hurricane, the term *feminist fiction* must be at least as unstable. But I suspect there's another reason. Even if we could provisionally agree that the vessels *feminist* and *fiction* are sound enough for this short trip, some fiction writers who confess to being feminists would still balk at climbing into the vessel *feminist fiction* with their treasured, vulnerable manuscripts. I sympathize. Who wants to capsize in shark-infested waters?

The first novelist I consult asks warily, "Feminist fiction—what exactly do you mean?"—as if I were setting a trap. With one breath she wants to be invited along on the trip, even resents a critic who once complained in print that her fiction was insufficiently political. But with her next breath she confides, "Frankly, I think people are turned off by the whole category. If they [or did she say *I*?] read a feminist novel it's *despite* not *because* it's feminist."

Again! Only this time it's a fiction writer saying it. "Really?" I ask, registering my surprise as I think of such feminist favorites as *The Color Purple* and *To the Lighthouse*. "People are turned off?"

And yet, I can't be all that surprised since I must admit that when strangers ask me what kind of novels I write, I don't always volunteer straight out, "feminist novels"—not unless I know who's asking, and why. Sometimes when it's Open Season on Ladies' Lit and the critics are out there pillorying feminists as polemicists ("that busy battalion of American women novelists who have been flooding the market with their crudely polemical morality tales of liberation," runs a typical tirade), I wouldn't mind slipping quietly away like some of my writing friends who leave town when their books are coming out to avoid seeing reviews—though in fact, as an activist, I feel duty bound to stand and fight. On the other hand, when I am credited with changing someone's life, whether blamed (as by the Ohio man who wrote that it was my fault his wife took off with the baby and left him after reading one of my novels) or thanked (as in the frequent letters from women telling me the stories of their lives), then I'll wear the label in the same spirit with which I wear one of my hundred political buttons to a demonstration—slightly uncomfortable about condensing my impossibly complicated views down to a phrase, but proud to lend my body to the cause. Since my own voice talks on in my books, I'm willing to submerge it temporarily in the unified roar of the crowd for the sake of something I believe in.

"Why do you suppose it turns people off?" I ask. But this question too is slightly disingenuous. In the unending game of Naming-the-Despised no one wants to be tagged *It* at the moment the music stops. Everyone scrambles for a safe seat. So, in another area, the acceptable name has passed from Person of Color to Black to Negro and back to Black and Person of Color again. I know perfectly well that whereas not so long ago many women writers bristled at being considered "women writers," dreading the label as limiting, disparaging, even dismissive, now, when, thanks to feminism, gender is no longer a legitimate category of dismissal in the arts, the new bugaboo seems to be the label "feminist writer," even among women who may no longer mind being called women writers or, for that matter, feminists.

Why?

Too—well—*political.*

"Don't you read feminist fiction, then?" I continue.

"Not if I can help it," replies my friend unabashedly. "Unless I happen to know it's good art."

I look at her, a sometime feminist who has occasionally expressed regret that she missed out on the high times of the movement. Why this presumption that feminist fiction is bad art? Badass maybe, but bad art? Not that I haven't read my share of preachy, pompous, dull, sentimental, haranguing, or unconvincing fiction, but I can't say it's been especially feminist. Assuming that good art and bad occur in feminist novels in about the same proportion as in any other type, I want on the contrary to presume for this discussion that we're talking only about the good-art ones. Why bother with the other kind at all? A serious discussion of any genre will involve the best, not the worst, of the type. I consider proposing that maybe a feminist novel is a novel that moves or delights one's feminist bones, which would mean it must be "good art." But I doubt my friend would buy it.

And then I see it overhead clinging to the wall, that scaly green lizard, Politics versus Art, looking down on us with its beady eyes and flicking its lightning tongue. I'm astonished at my friends— political and engaged!—for still harboring that peculiarly American presumption that politics and art don't mix. Or that when they do mix, what comes out is poison propaganda. As if feminist fiction meant putting the needs of feminism over those of fiction; as if feminism were more narrowly ideological than visionary; as if there could be fiction without political implications; as if one invariably had to choose. Why is it that in other countries novelists (particularly celebrated male ones) are expected to explore political questions in their work and express opinions on every political subject without compromising their art, are even looked to as spokespeople, but not here in the United States? Here, it's widely presumed that you must choose either art or politics, not both. Given the suspicion surrounding the artist who dreams of political consequence, this very presumption may itself produce constricting pressure on artistic integrity equal to the presumed pressure produced by political commitment. Alas, most fiction writers I know meekly, if regretfully, accept the necessity of the choice and choose the safety of art—particularly if the politics in question are feminist.

Because, let's face it, feminism—initially perceived as daring, sexy, rebellious, gutsy, new—is now suspected in certain circles of being tainted, like food that's been around too long: even if it's still all right, better not take a chance on it, better be safe and toss it out. I recognize the distaste in my friend's response, her fear of having her work contaminated by association with two potent contaminants, women and politics, both implied by feminism, and to her mind inviting dismissal of her work as trivial, as ideological, as boring. If it's feminist, she intimates, it won't be considered art.

How did this dissociation happen? Sadly I recognize the trivializing taint as the very one that has long infected everything associated with women, from motherhood to makeup, that feminism was founded to eliminate. I believe this is why many women, particularly the young, even those with fairly feminist politics, shy away from the term *feminist*: it is too closely associated with—oh, you know—women. What irony! After its bold strike for wholeness and health, feminism, instead of cleansing women of the taint, as it set out to do, itself became tainted, until now, again, fiction writers like my friend, ambitious for as large an audience as possible, avoid an association of their work with that compromising parochial word.

(If this avoidance is much less true of critics and academics than of artists, it's probably because they are not only permitted but required to deal in ideas, while artists, amazingly, are not. The highest praise T. S. Eliot could give Henry James was that he had "a mind so fine no idea could violate it." There are quite a few excellent journals devoted to feminist theory, hardly any to feminist fiction. Besides, some feminist critics have tenure.)

The troublesome suspicion between feminist art and politics, writers and activists, has actually gone both ways. Back in the early days of the women's liberation movement, it was widely thought that anyone who wrote about the new feminist ideas, especially for a large audience, was probably "ripping off the movement" for personal gain. As part of the debate over individualism within feminism, some people held that since the ideas of the movement belong equally to everyone, not just to those who write them down, any writing feminist ought to leave her work unsigned. Others went further and thought that since no one has a right to speak for anyone else (yes, feminists were saying that way back then!), and writers are often treated by the world as spokespeople, writers should keep (contradiction in terms) quiet and not write at all. Kate Millett, Robin Morgan, and Ellen Willis themselves did not escape the ire (and envy?) of the movement. This peculiar historical anomaly seems almost incomprehensible today; who in the movement would dream of criticizing Mary Gordon, say, or Barbara Ehrenreich for publishing under their own names? Yet at a time when, because of the encouragement of the movement, many women were for the first time developing the confidence and analytic skills necessary to write, hardly any feminist writer I know escaped a certain uneasiness about publishing feminist work. This was true even of fiction, though fiction aroused less suspicion in the movement than did theory— perhaps because on the surface fiction seems more personal, idiosyncratic, and to ideologues even frivolous.

But this peculiar idea that if your writing embodies feminism you can't be a loyal feminist seems to me precisely as absurd as the complementary notion that if your writing embodies feminism you can't be a good fiction writer. Isn't it obvious that your best writing will embody what you know best and feel most passionate about?—

ALIX KATES SHULMAN

that if you have feminist values, your fiction will probably have feminist values, too? Why would you ever have to choose?

Just as I was beginning to worry that I might be the only fiction writer I know who isn't nervous about being described as a feminist one, another writer, Grace Paley, whose large and devoted following is not particularly associated with feminism, outdid me in her confident embrace of the term. "Yes!" she responded to the question, Do you consider yourself a feminist writer?—almost before it was out of my mouth. Far from skulking about in fear of the *F*-word, she takes the largest view of feminist fiction, large enough to include not only her own work (which she twinklingly allows was feminist even before there was a movement) but the work of certain writers she most admires, including some who decline the label, like Christa Wolf and Doris Lessing. "But that doesn't mean their work isn't feminist," she argues. Revered by men and women alike, and heaped with literary honors, her access to readers is not endangered. "I'd argue with them. I'd say their work is definitely feminist, whether they say so or not."

("And I'd say *her* work, though wonderful, is *not* feminist, no matter what *she* says," appended another friend, a critic, *sotto voce*.)

So—some say they aren't who are, some say they are who aren't, and some aren't saying. Overhearing us, another writer enters the discussion to insist that the very question is counterproductive, that any representation of the writer's work is misrepresentation. Instead, she insists, people should just read the books, allowing each fiction to fall where it may, like Pick-Up-Sticks, and the hell with what -*ist* it is. More anxious than the others I've been talking to, younger and less successful, her voice is unusually soft for this crowd. Not that she would deny her feminism, she says in an aside, no more than she would deny being Jewish; still, what's the point in being "ghettoized"? She's against all labels, which, she says, are always used against us.

Finally, I consult a feminist critic I much admire, a smart, avid reader and teacher of fiction. She dismisses the large questions and definitions as "no longer interesting" following upon fifteen years of sophisticated, often brilliant, feminist literary criticism. Instead, she proposes that the smallest and least mushy category, the most neglected and thereby the most interesting one, is Feminist Fiction with capital *Fs*—that is, fiction by political women for whom the contemporary women's movement was one of the major experiences of their lives, an experience leaving its traces in virtually all their thought and work. This, she contends, is probably what most people think of when they hear the term feminist fiction, anyway: politically engaged fiction. I wonder: is this the reason for the purported turn-off reported by my informants? For though feminism is everywhere alive, the political movement is, at least in the United States, quiescent. Much more than feminist ideas, which turn up everywhere nowadays, it's the movement that currently suffers image trouble.

Together we review the fiction we know and come up with a short list of Feminist Works, including books by Margaret Atwood, Angela Carter, Marilyn French, Ursula K. Le Guin, Maxine Hong Kingston, Marge Piercy, Joanna Russ, Jane Rule, Alice Walker, Fay Weldon, Monique Wittig—but I won't go on. Some of these writers are acquaintances and might be distressed by my naming names. Better to risk their feeling slighted at being left off the list than exposed by being put on it; they may be grateful to me later. I suspect that even they (even I?) would prefer to be considered not by their gender or their politics but simply as writers, if that were only possible. One of the advantages of fiction over theory, after all, is its unarguable particularity, with all characters, events, ideas, and opinions drawn solely from the imagination, where any resemblance to others is purely coincidental. No forced outings in my article! I'll protect my sources and let you each compile your own list.

Still, the list my friend and I compiled seemed surprisingly short. Why? Perhaps because revolutions, social or political, may be just too noisy and intense to give rise to an extensive literature, which must be created in hours and years of reflective calm. From experience I know well that activists' energies are directed outward, writers' energies inward. It's probably as easy to record a revolution from the midst of it when everyone is working at fever pitch as it is to write a novel standing in a rush-hour subway train. Plus, as Lenin said on the eve of the October Revolution, laying aside the incomplete manuscript of his *State and Revolution*, "it is more pleasant and useful to go through 'the experience of the revolution' than to write about it."

But Lenin was not a novelist. And not every artist transformed by the great social movements of her time is confounded by the oppressive either/or of art and politics. In *Meridian*, her feminist novel about the civil rights movement, Alice Walker offers another possibility. Speaking in the voice of the artist, she writes:

> *Perhaps it will be my part to walk behind the real revolutionaries— those who know they must spill blood in order to help the poor and the black . . . And when they stop to wash off the blood . . . I will come forward and sing from memory songs they will need once more to hear. For it is the song of the people, transformed by the experiences of each generation, that holds them together, and if any part of it is lost the people suffer and are without soul.*

In the end, it was not one of my literary friends but a well-read scientist, Naomi Weisstein, who came up with the description of feminist fiction I plan to live with. (A longtime feminist working in another field, she doesn't worry about the consequences of publicity in this one, so I dare to reveal her name.) Sensible, expansive, and illuminating, her description allows me to include on my list a wide range of writers I admire, from the past as well as the present, without unduly stretching the term. Here it is:

> *Feminist fiction is fiction that does not admire patriarchy or accept its ideology. Nor does it portray its male characters as naturally more exciting, more important, or more valuable than its female*

*characters. In addition, the female characters are valued enough to be presented in their full humanity, whether they be villains or heroes, and the sympathetic female characters are neither necessarily nice nor necessarily beautiful. In this way, feminist fiction challenges the patriarchal belief in the fixed and eternal nature of men and women.*

You get the drift. Naomi's generous, if negative, description leaves the imagination free of restrictions and is clear enough to counter the prejudice I keep bumping into. Who could object? True, it is one of the looser ones; but, then, one of the most hopeful aspects of the women's movement is its struggle to be widely inclusive. In each of its particulars, Naomi's description closely resembles the vision that inspired me to become both a feminist and a novelist in the first place. Without that vision, instead of soberly declaring myself a feminist novelist whatever the consequences (for I can't recant and refuse to choose), I would probably still be playing the game of Name Tag and scrambling like crazy when the music stops.

# WOMEN WRITERS
# IN THE BEAT GENERATION

I know that I shall be the sea
And the mother
And never me.
Wait
I am here
Under the sea
Recognize me

—Sally Stern, "Wait I've Been This Way Before,"
in *The Beat Scene*

WHEN I WAS DOING RESEARCH for my 1978 novel *Burning Questions*, about the rise of the women's liberation movement, I was shocked to discover that the young radical feminists of the 1970s regarded the Beat period with a certain idealized nostalgia. What was shocking was their assumption that those women in black leotards and thong sandals who were associated with the Beat writers in the flourishing bohemia of lower Manhattan in the 1950s were somehow their predecessors in the struggle for women's liberation. That image certainly didn't accord with my experience. It's true that the Beat movement was liberatory—but not really for women. As one of the many young women who had fled to Greenwich Village in 1953 at the age of twenty seeking adventure, significance, and escape from a set of materialistic, conformist values, I knew first-hand that the popular view was mistaken. In fact, however stimulating and exciting it was to be in the midst of the new jazz, art, and poetry, it was every bit as oppressive to women and as dominated by outright misogyny as square culture—and in some ways worse, since you weren't allowed to complain.

So when I tried to recreate that important moment of our cultural history in my novel, to prepare myself I read as widely as I could in the literature of the women Beats, hoping to test my own experience against theirs. And what I quickly discovered was that with one important exception, the poet Diane di Prima, there were no Beat women writers to speak of.

The few women whose work does occasionally appear in the early anthologies of Beat writing (and I'm talking here about 2 out of 25, 4 out of 44, that order of magnitude) or whose names figure in histories of the period were imported from other sensibilities, eras, and schools (Denise Levertov, Barbara Guest, Jean Garigue). Or they stopped writing and quickly passed into obscurity, like Sally Stern, whose poem from *The Beat Scene* I use here as my epigraph because it protests the very invisibility I'm talking about.

I did, however, in my search for Beat women writers find several memoirs of the period, written by women situated, because of their close association with Beat men, at the very center of the Beat movement; and although it took decades for most of them to write and publish their memoirs, they do help throw light on the vexing question of why there are so few Beat women writers when previous flowerings of bohemia in lower Manhattan, from the turn of the century on through the 1920s, had featured so many notable women artists and rebels, like Isadora Duncan, Emma Goldman, Crystal Eastman, Susan Glaspell, Dorothy Day, Edna St. Vincent Millay? Why, as Hettie Jones, ex-wife of LeRoi Jones (later as a black militant renamed Amiri Baraka), repeatedly asks throughout her book, did the wives of writers and artists of the new consciousness so readily subvert their own ambitions and desires to those of their men? The writers whose memoirs form the basis of my discussion are, in order of publication: first Diane di Prima, our exception to the rule, the only one of them who is an authentic Beat poet in her own right, whose long out-of-print underground classic, the 1969 *Memoirs of a Beatnik*, was finally reissued in 1988; next, Bonnie Bremser, wife of Beat poet Ray Bremser (*Troia*, or *For Love of Ray*, 1969); Carolyn Cassady, wife of Neal Cassady [Kerouac's Dean Moriarty] (*Heart Beat*, 1976 and *Off the Road*, 1990); Joyce Johnson, lover of Jack Kerouac (*Minor Characters*, 1983); and most recently, Hettie Jones (*How I Became Hettie Jones*, 1990). I'll speak a bit about each of them later, but first I want to discuss the background situation these women shared among the Beats.

These memoirists were college educated, they had enough rebelliousness and personal ambition to draw them to the Village—to put them at the right time in the right place to develop their talents—yet, for all the ambition and formidable talent of several of them, for the most part they seemed hardly better able to escape or defy the feminine mystique they had presumably fled than the rest of the country. Why?

My answer has to do with the absence of any hint of feminism even in bohemia, and worse, the unselfconscious incorporation of misogyny in the Beat ideology itself. Following decades of organized and militant feminism, bohemians of the 1920s, men and women alike, revolting against the notion that woman's place is in the home, consciously supported sexual equality and women's emancipation as explicit goals, even if they had a hard time living out these ideals. But by the time the Beats were ascendant, the postwar renewal of mandatory domesticity, sexual repression, and gender rigidity, in opposition to which the Beats defined their values, had so routed feminism from the national ideology that it lapsed even in bohemia. Despite its libratory philosophy and elevation of sex, both homosexual and heterosexual, to what John Tytell called "the one and only important thing in life," the Beat ideology claimed liberation for men, not women.

Why feminism disappeared is outside my scope here; instead, I want to explore the consequences of its disappearance. (Nor do I want to assign blame; as Diane di Prima said in a recent interview, "the men in the scene had no way to realize how sexist they were because that was the time.")

**Against gender rigidity** the Beats, a primarily male society, posed homosexuality, entailing what Ginsberg has called "the break-through of the feminine within us . . . bringing out the tender, tear-ful, sensitive aspect of men." But not a loosening of gender roles for women or a redefinition of masculine and feminine. (At the end of the parties in Kerouac's novels, for example, a woman often comes in to do the cleaning up.) **Against sexual repression**, the Beats, like earlier bohemians, posed sexual freedom, but—also, like their pre-decessors—it was not the freedom generally desired by women, for often the elevation of sex meant love-em-and-leave-em when it came to women. (As Kerouac once said, "I wasn't trying to create any new kind of consciousness or anything like that. We were just a bunch of guys who were trying to get laid.") **Against materialism**, the Beats posed mysticism—plus a rejection of consumerism and a denigra-tion of regular nine-to-five jobs (for men, though not for the women who frequently worked as clericals to support the men); for men a regular job was "a slave," "embarrassing and aberrant" to have. For women, says Hettie Jones, a job sometimes had a different mean-ing—independence. **Against domesticity**, the Beats posed an ideal of constant motion, pursued without the regular company of women. (Joyce Johnson laments that if she hinted at accompanying Kerouac on the road, he would "stop me by saying that what I really wanted were babies. That was what all women wanted and what I wanted too, even though I said I didn't.")

The Housewife was demonized by the Beats, no less than in the popular culture of the square world of the period, as typically a devouring subverter of the freedom of men and the life-force of artists. Home and family appeared no less confining to the bohemian predecessors of the Beats, but there was an important difference: Instead of seeing the bourgeois family as a prison for both men and women alike, Beats tended to identify women with the family and see them not as prisoners but as prison guards. Consequently, Beat men of the 1950s urged emancipation *from* women rather than *for* them, perceiving them as the embodiment of family and the guardians of sex, domesticators out to trap them into commitments, or sexual adversaries whose powers must be overcome. Beat men, married or not, took to the road to escape the women and find the girls. Jack Duluoz, narrator of Kerouac's *Visions of Cody*, says: "Her cunt is sweet, you get to it via white lace panties, and she be fine. This is almost all I can say about almost all girls."

The comic strip images of Dagwood and Blondie, or Maggie and Jiggs, with the husband meekly tiptoeing into the house at night carrying his shoes afraid of discovery by the all-powerful wife, usually waiting to clobber him, was taken over whole by the Beats. A woman concerned about her image did all she could to avoid being anything like Blondie. In her memoir Hettie Jones recounts that after she had her first child, LeRoi went out drinking every night, leaving her at home taking care of the baby.

One evening as he was leaving with his friend the poet Frank O'Hara she reports: "I threw my arms around [LeRoi] and out of my mouth sprang 'Don't be late.' Beside me Frank stiffened. But I already knew what I'd done. 'How's that for a line,' I said. Frank looked amazed. 'I thought you were serious,' he said." What a bind to be in—expected to take all the traditional wifely responsibilities, confined to that role, but at the same time despised for acting like a wife.

One of the best examples I know of this tension is the 1959 Beat film, "Pull My Daisy," directed by Robert Frank with screenplay and narration by Jack Kerouac, starring Kerouac, Allen Ginsberg, Gregory Corso, and others. The film shows a typical goofy day in the life of a group of Beat buddies in the Lower East Side loft of one of them, named Milo, and the plot, such as it is, reproduces the standard Blondie-Dagwood, Maggie-Jiggs scenario. The free-spirited Beats are all bursting with poetry, while Milo's wife (played by actress Delphine Seyrig, later superb in "Last Year at Marienbad"), who has to see to the practical details of taking care of the kids, taking them to school, serving the food, entertaining, keeping some order in the house, is pictured as the eternal spoil sport, though she's a painter herself. The climax of the film occurs when Milo successfully sneaks down the stairs away from her to join his buddies in freedom. The mood is certainly playful and light-hearted enough, but the victim-blaming subtext is grim.

Where did this attitude leave the women? Young 1950s women fleeing to bohemia to live as rebels, and hoping as much as the men to escape sexual repression and stultifying convention, found themselves unsuspectingly rushing into the arms of their foes. At the very cultural moment when women most urgently needed the power and perspective of feminism, bohemia itself, once a refuge, turned out to be a blockhouse of misogyny. Bohemia's vaunted sexual freedom could be had only on the men's terms. Trapped in a cruel self-fulfilling prophecy, women soon discovered that the more elusive and restless the men, the more abject they themselves must behave, capitulating to the men's worst view of them in their attempt to prove themselves worthy.

Paul Goodman, the late poet, novelist, and anarchist intellectual, asks in *Growing Up Absurd*, that cult book of the early 1960s, "What is in it for the women who accompany the Beats?" since "Beat culture . . . is essentially for men." He proposes that women may be maternal, may be Muse or Model to the Beat artist, or, finally, may be "themselves Beats, disaffected from status standards. Perhaps they have left an unlucky marriage, have had an illegitimate child, have fallen in love with a Negro and found little support or charity 'in' society. They might then choose a life among those more tolerant, and find meaning in it by posing for them or typing their manuscripts." This he proposes without a trace of irony.

Faced with the inescapable dilemma of yearning for acceptance in a misogynistic culture, what was a woman to do? Short of remaining unattached—difficult in a world where women were validated only by men—any course a Beat woman chose must include some basic self-contempt. Trapped inside the body of the enemy, sooner or later she would discover that no matter what she said or did, to the men whose values she espoused she represented what she had thought to rebel against. If they stood up to the men they were Bitches, if they lay down for them they were Patsies, either way subverting their own desires. Winning was losing: di Prima writes in her first book of poems ("More or Less Love Poems"): "I have the upper hand / but if I keep it / I'll lose the circulation in one arm."

Beat men, even the married ones, turned for emotional intensity not to women, whom they seldom considered colleagues or equals, but to other men. If a woman tried to escape suspicion by making ever fewer demands, the more tenuous would be her connection to her lover. In *Memoirs of a Beatnik*, di Prima writes, when her lover has to split to New Orleans, "Our code, our eternal, tiresome rule of Cool, would have made it impossible for me to say ['I'm going with you'] without blowing our entire scene, retrospectively even, blowing what had gone before, so that if I had indeed gone with Rudy all the magic would have gone out of our coming together." Although Beat was a cult of spontaneity and heart, of feeling over intellect, feelings of attachment between the sexes were fatally uncool.

This then is the predicament. Each of the memoirs I've been looking at portrays a very different accommodation to the problem of being Beat and female. Though each fails in its way, all are revealing, each epitomizing one of the few roles available to women among the Beats: di Prima is the Artist, the exception, one-of-the-boys; Johnson is the Groupie; the other three are all Wives (and of all Beat women, Beat wives seem the most hopelessly compromised): one the Mother (Cassidy), one the Whore (Bremser), one the Helpmate (Jones). Let me briefly describe them.

Carolyn Cassady is Mrs. Beat and mother to the three children of Mr. Beat—Neal Cassady, legendary coast-to-coast driver, model for Kerouac's, Ginsberg's and Ken Kesey's heroes. Her short memoir, *Heart Beat: My Life with Jack and Neal*, covers the year 1952–53, when Kerouac moved into the attic of the Cassadys' California house and they lived in a ménage a trois; it was made into a Hollywood movie in 1980. In 1991, a much expanded memoir came out: *Off the Road*.

Her way to deal with the Beat/woman dilemma is simply to accept without complaint her inferior status as all-suffering wife. She is the caretaker, outsider, Mother. When friends bring peyote to the house, she declines to partake in order to "be able to function normally—if anyone required help," and admits that "the bohemian scene now was less compatible to me than when I'd been younger." Although she tries to present herself as the center of a glamorous ménage a trois, throughout her book she continually reveals how alienated and excluded from Beat life she is made to feel.

When Jack and Neal go out to party or "shut themselves up in the attic" she feels like a "neglected household drudge." But once Jack starts sleeping with her at Neal's suggestion,

*I began a season of singing days and nights, I was a part of all they did now and I felt like the star of the show. I felt I was a real contributor for once. My housework and baby care had a purpose; it was needed and appreciated. I was functioning as a female, and my men were men. . . .*

*They were such different types; how lucky could a girl get? Each was being himself, and I served whichever was in residence according to their individual requirements.*

*While I performed my household duties the men would read each other excerpts from their writing in progress or bring out Spengler, Proust or Shakespeare to read aloud, accompanied by energetic discussions and appraisals. I was happy just listening to them and filling their coffee cups. Yet I never felt left out. They'd address remarks to me and include me in the group with smiles, pats and requests for opinions or to moderate an argument.*

And though her self-esteem temporarily rises under the attention provided by the new arrangement, her basic sense of exclusion persists throughout the book. For example, when Ginsberg addresses a letter directly to her she is amazed and "overjoyed to be thus recognized as an official member of the clan." She is "staggered" when Jack invites her to visit him in Mexico. When she accepts the invitation and Neal gets sulky she remarks, "I could hardly credit my senses. Because of me? Neal was feeling rejected by me? And he cared?" In the end, she decides not to join Jack in Mexico. "It didn't fit my idea of motherhood, and it was a pretty serious affront to my marriage vows," so when Jack inevitably backs out she can act relieved. "Poor, dear Jack," she muses in her fantasies, "I had already pretty well decided that married life with Jack on a daily basis would never work."

Years later when Jack is gone, the kids are somewhat older, and Neal is in jail, she has to choose between the roles of Wife and Mother. At last she rises above the passivity, not for herself but for the children, as she puts the role of Mother first by refusing to forfeit the house to pay Neal's bail. "It was a rending decision," she writes elsewhere, one that enrages Neal, but, "with three small children, I didn't think I had the right." Going to work to support the family she considers her "final admission that I must abandon my dreams for ever being truly his wife"—in her mind the ultimate sacrifice.

Bonnie Bremser's memoir, *Troia (For Love of Ray)*, for all its Beat syntax, language, and rhythms, and its depiction of a life of sex, drugs, and constant motion, tells a story of another kind of wifely self-sacrifice. (Though Bremser is a flamboyant, rebellious, impulsive kid—no household drudge like Cassidy—her husband, older and tougher, can handle her. No wonder that unlike Cassidy she is Wife first, Mother second.)

When the book opens, Bonnie, Ray, and their baby Rachel are in Mexico on the run. Six months after they married he was jailed and she pregnant; now he is a fugitive from parole from a New Jersey prison. Ray, who embodies the extreme macho idealized criminal side of Beat mythology, nags Bonnie to shut Rachel up, or else he goes off by himself. The family stays on the move, hiding out in cheap hotels or with friends, getting constantly stoned, until one day, dead broke, Ray forces Bonnie to turn tricks. From then on, every afternoon she tries to resist, every night Ray forces her out again, sometimes hustling customers for her. With few exceptions she hates the work and the Mexican johns, but she reluctantly goes along since, as she writes, "it was nothing but me and the general public between us and starvation and the jailhouse." She rationalizes that she used to sleep around anyway, so why not do it "for love of Ray" who she thinks is "surely poetry's representative in the flesh."

Eventually Ray is picked up and deported to a Texas jail. Loyal wife Bonnie leaves the baby with a friend, hustles her way across the border, then hustles to get Ray sprung. Once out, he arranges to give the baby up in order to facilitate their getaway back to Mexico. Bonnie is badly shaken by this event, but since she can't be successful both as a mother and a breadwinning wife (i.e., prostitute), she accepts the inevitable, hoping Rachel may also benefit. Even supercool Ray admits in an unguarded moment "I feel sick about the whole thing, baby, yeah, me, too, Ray"—but he steadies her hand so she can sign the papers giving up Rachel.

As soon as they run out of their getaway money, Ray sends Bonnie back out on the street, while he writes. If she tries to defy him he beats her up. "He maintains it is good for a chick to get pounded on once and [sic] awhile for it increases the circulation and makes her pretty."

She complains that "Ray was out of the hotel a lot, writing poems, he says, and often didn't come back all night," while she lies in bed apathetic and disgusted "at the apparently permanent occupation of fucking a bunch of guys I didn't like . . . to get money for us to continue this way. It has no rewards for me, I am alone, lonely, bugged, feeling more and more unloved, as if each trick I turn is a negative score on the happiness list." Even though this is her book, not his, like a good wife she catches herself up, stops complaining and tells us, "Oh shit, let me try to dig up a little joy here to interject—and in real life there was once and often joy here and there, simple stolen joy, get high on pot, and go out and eat in a restaurant . . . look at the movie magazines and dig the chicks. . . ." Here you can hear the imitation of Beat writing, but the mood is entirely different, the joy is fake. Their fights escalate, but since she is the breadwinner, she muses, in another reversal, "Ray knows he is trapped with me."

Despite her anguish over losing her child, and depression over her own lot, the book's major point is that love justifies all. "Here is the way I really am," writes Bonnie in the foreword: "My heart belonged to Ray since the day I met him in Washington, that is the basis of my life." She also ends with this love refrain, though Ray's own book of poems, *Blowing Mouth*, published half a dozen years later, is dedicated to a different young woman: "For Judith Johnson / Forever . . .").

Hettie Jones, nee Cohen, the third Beat wife to write a memoir and by far the most reflective and accomplished of the three, is at the beginning ostensibly as ambitious as her husband, Roi. They meet working similar jobs on a record magazine; soon Hettie moves to *Partisan Review* as circulation manager (where, incidentally, she gets Roi published); together the Joneses put out their own journal *Yugen*, "a new consciousness in arts and letters." But once they are married and have a child, everything changes rapidly. She realizes that "there were different transformations awaiting us. He would remain, like any man of any race, exactly as he was, augmented," whereas she would "lose my past to share his," particularly since her family renounced her for marrying a black man. She feels herself increasingly relegated to the sidelines reserved for wives, mothers, and women artists. He goes out every night, taking up with a string of women, while she is a "thrumming blinking bleating switchboard." Yet she is forbidden by the prevailing rules of cool to make any domestic or sexual demands on him: when she objects to his womanizing he temporarily moves out, even though she's pregnant again, and when she retaliates with her own affairs, he rages. Ashamed of "burying [her] talent in a napkin," and subordinating her own ambitions to her husband's—even though she continues to write in secret, design and sew her own clothes, dance, and act in the avant-garde theater (in a play LeRoi never bothers to attend)— she mourns over "poor discarded Hettie *Cohen*. With all her grand ambition, all she'd ever 'become' was Hettie Jones." That LeRoi is also disappointed in her is especially galling.

With the swell of the civil rights movement and the new militancy of the 1960s, Hettie recognizes that LeRoi "couldn't stay King of the Hill by standing still." After seven years of marriage and two children, his successful plays about race move him to the center of the Black Power movement, and he feels he must leave her. The scene is searing. She writes: "I could feel it coming, like an awful tide. I said 'Why?' and then there it was: 'Because you're white.' "

Comparing her father and her husband, she observes: "Both these men . . . first loved me for myself, and then discarded me when that self no longer fit their daughter/wife image."

Written since the women's movement, Jones's important and moving memoir ponders the predicament of bohemian wives of the 1950s in the reflected light of two decades of feminist analysis, and details the circumstances and feelings that made it virtually impossible for her to find the confidence and the time to pursue her own ambitions amidst the proliferating responsibilities of breadwinner, publisher, mother of two, homemaker, seamstress, hostess, secretary to her husband, wife. But instead of forgiving herself, she writes, "In retrospect there's some terrible shame—how could we?"—assuming total responsibility, as if women's liberation could have been accomplished, absent a movement, by will alone. This attitude is not surprising when she has before her the example of the exceptional Diane di Prima, who during the period Hettie was married to LeRoi also bore LeRoi a child and collaborated with him on a magazine, but seemed to have no trouble writing and publishing her poems. Hettie writes: "Diane was everything I wasn't. To begin she was single."

Joyce Johnson also writes from much later, the 1980s, safely outside the Beat subculture, with her lover Kerouac long dead and herself an accomplished novelist, successful editor, mother. However, her beautifully written memoir, *Minor Characters*, lacks Jones's feminist consciousness. During her intermittent youthful affair with the elusive Kerouac, who would crash with her whenever he was in New York, she was working on a novel of her own with Henry James, not Kerouac, her literary model; yet, she admits, "I always wanted to be with [Jack] more than I wanted to be at the typewriter." Her stance is that of a savvy, cautious observer. "How Beat could I actually be, holding down a steady office job and writing a novel about an ivy league college girl on the verge of parting with her virginity?"

Still, so seductive did she find the Beats and their pursuit of "intensity for its own sake" that she was tempted to become some artist's "old lady"—"straighten him out a little, clean up the studio, contribute to the rent, have a baby or two, become one of those weary, quiet, self-sacrificing, widely respected women brought by their men to the Cedar on occasional Saturday nights in their limp thrift-shop dresses made interesting with beads. Even a very young woman can achieve old-ladyhood, become the mainstay of someone else's self-destructive genius." What saves her is not a sense of self-preservation but being in love with Jack, who has already had enough old ladies, thank you. Had Kerouac wanted her she would have leaped, even at 22; both Cassady and Johnson describe him as one of the sweetest of men. It took her years of separations, uncertainty, jealousy and rejections by him before reaching the point where "what you've been bearing all along suddenly becomes unbearable," and she abandons all hope of winning him.

Of the five memoirists, Johnson is the least engulfed in Beat values, the most detached, never so deeply involved that she couldn't pull out without forfeit. Yet, puzzlingly, she seems to view this more as her loss than her gain. The dominant tone of her elegant memoir is of wistful regret that she was never really accepted by the Beats and never managed to penetrate "as completely as I longed to" that inner world from which women were excluded.

Diane di Prima's exuberant bisexual romp, *Memoirs of a Beatnik*, I've saved for the end, since it is the only celebration of Beat culture written by a woman, and di Prima is the only woman writer I know of to escape the double standard and genuinely embrace Beat values, and to be accepted by the Beats, as if she were one of the boys. A founder and editor of several Beat journals, organizer of some of the original poetry readings, an accomplished and prolific poet whose relative obscurity compared to the men with whom she is usually associated is something of a scandal today, di Prima confronts the dangers of female subservience with bravado, accepting the burden of proof that she is no mere woman. Not that the protagonist of her memoir escapes the Beat woman's dilemma, but her solution to it is to stay cool, itself a Beat response. "Your air was casual, and your face betrayed no emotion at all. Even in bed . . . the game is Cool." She will be as cool as any man, beat them at their own game, never become emotionally vulnerable.

*Memoirs of a Beatnik*, though not strictly a memoir, commissioned as it was by Olympia Press as pornography and first published as such in 1969, has been praised as a true evocation of the period. Since making your living through pornography and having lots of gooey sex are both part of the "easy, unself-conscious Bohemian" life di Prima is trying to portray in this ficto-biographical novel cum memoir (with, I suspect, imaginary cocks but real names), it is not inappropriate that the slender volume has crammed detailed descriptions of 25 different couplings plus three orgies in among the "tiny perfect memories" that soon begin to take over the writing. (The sex is pre-AIDS, the consciousness pre-feminist, the life pre-hippy, the style an always energetic but sometimes uncertain combination of spoof, satire, and nostalgia.) After six chapters of sex description that for all di Prima's poetic ingenuity does eventually begin to pall, the writer steps up to recreate her memories and impressions of a moment in Manhattan when she was seventeen, "the dance was the Fish and the game was Cool."

*It was a time when there was only a small handful of us— perhaps forty or fifty in the city—who knew what we knew; who raced about in Levis and work shirts, smoked dope, dug the new jazz, and spoke a bastardization of the black argot . . . Our chief concern was to keep our integrity (much time and energy went into defining the concept of the 'sellout') and to keep our cool: a hard, clean edge and definition in the midst of the terrifying indifference and sentimentality around us—'media mush.' We looked to each other for comfort, for praise, for love, and shut out the rest of the world.*

Di Prima knows the danger of attachment as well as any Beat male: "It is usually a good thing to be the woman of many men at once, or to be one of the many women on one man's scene, or to be one of the many women in a household with many men, and the scene between all of you shifting and ambiguous. What is not good, what is claustrophobic and deadening after a while, is the one-one relationship . . . Live with one man and you begin to have a claim on him. Live with five, and you have the same claim, but it is spread out, ambiguous, undefined." This sounds like a familiar Beat position, but with a difference: she's worried about making claims (as women do) rather than about feeling claimed (as men do). And instead of rejecting such claims, as Beat men might, she wants to diffuse them.

The climax of the book occurs when a friend brings her Ginsberg's *Howl*. Reading it, she realizes something new was about to happen. "The phrase 'breaking ground' kept coming into my head. I knew that this Allen Ginsberg, whoever he was, had been breaking ground for all of us, though I had no idea yet what that meant, how far it would take us—I sensed that Allen was only, could only be, the vanguard of a much larger thing. All the people, who, like me, had hidden and sulked, writing down what they knew for a small handful of friends, waiting with only a slight bitterness for the thing to end, for man's era to draw to a close in a blaze of radiation—all these would now step forward and say their pieces. I was high and delighted—a new era had begun."

She celebrates the new era with a final, hilarious orgy the night Ginsberg, Kerouac and Peter Orlovsky come to visit her and her roommates. But for all the fun, when at the end of the book she decides to have a baby, she's savvy enough to know that for her yet another new era has begun. It's hard to be cool with a baby.

Most of her poetry is written post-baby and tells a somewhat different story from that of the memoir. Though there is not a word of complaint about woman's predicament in the memoir, which is, after all, the fantasy of a persona, written presumably for a male audience, her poetry from that period complains of the need to hide feelings and of sexism.

I will give you one example of her poetry, from a poem called "The Quarrel": "You know I thought I've got work to do too sometimes. In fact I probably have just as fucking much work to do as you do . . . / I am sick I said to the woodpile of doing dishes. I am just as lazy as you. Maybe lazier . . . / Just because I happen to be a chick I thought. / . . . I got up and went into the kitchen to do the dishes. . . . I'll never say anything because it's so fucking uncool to talk about it— / Hey hon Mark yelled at me from the living room. It says here Picasso produces fourteen hours a day."

Not that the Beat bards don't deserve everyone's gratitude for making public readings popular, reviving poetry as performance with "their boy songs," as Grace Paley sometimes called them, for loosening up the heterosexual stranglehold, for rejecting bourgeois values, and for enriching literature with many treasures. But on the Woman Question they were no better than those who embraced the established values the Beats rebelled against and were considerably worse than many of their bohemian forebears. Allen Ginsberg asks in a recent interview, "Were we responsible for the lack of outstanding genius in the women we knew? I don't think so." But I don't think it's just a matter of "genius." Not that I want to hold the men responsible, but you can't blame the victims either for their diminished capacity. The Beat ideology made it almost impossible for the women to develop their talents because, despite their desires and sometimes brave attempts to live as rebels (like Hettie Jones's), except for di Prima, they felt themselves to be failures, and their men demanded that they come first. In fact, in relation to their men, the lives they describe seem in some ways not all that different from those of their non-Beat counterparts: Cassady resembles a conventional suburban housewife; Bremser a run of the mill street hustler with her pimp; Jones an abandoned helpmate, Johnson a lovesick girl. The major difference is that for a time each believed her ordinary life so redeemed by her attachment to a glamorous, exceptional man that it could no longer be said to be ordinary. But given that the men in their potentially liberating quest allowed no equal place for women among them, the redemption fails to convince. The saddest part is that it even fails to convince the women themselves.

## REFERENCES

*Memoirs of a Beatnik*, Diane di Prima, Olympia Press, 1969 (republished by Last Gasp Press, CA, 1988).

*Troia*, Bonnie Bremser, Croton Press, NY, 1969 (republished as *For Love of Ray*, London Magazine Editions, 1971).

*Heart Beat: My Life with Jack and Neal*, Carolyn Cassady, Creative Arts Book Co., Berkeley, 1976; *Off the Road: My Years with Cassady, Kerouac, and Ginsberg*, Morrow, 1990 (Penguin, 1991).

*Minor Characters: the Romantic Odyssey of a Woman in the Beat Generation*, Joyce Johnson, Houghton Mifflin, 1983.

*How I Became Hettie Jones*, Hettie Jones, Dutton, 1990 (Penguin, 1991).

*Autobiography of LeRoi Jones*, Amiri Baraka, Freundlich Books, 1984.

*Growing up Absurd*, Paul Goodman, Random House, 1960.

*Down and In: Life in the Underground*, Ronald Sukenick, Macmillan, 1987.

*The Beats*, ed. by Seymour Krim, Fawcett, 1960. In this important poetry anthology, out of 25 poets 2 are women (Brigid Mumaghan and Diane di Prima). In the 1960 Grove Press anthology *New American Poetry*, ed. by Donald M. Allen, 4 out of 44 poets are women: Denise Levertov, Helen Adam, Madeline Gleason, and Barbara Guest—not one of them a Beat.

*Four Young Lady Poets*, ed. by LeRoi and Hettie Jones, Corinth Press, 1961, including Diane di Prima, Rochelle Owens, Diane Wakoski, and Barbara Moraff. The book was duly criticized, in the journal *Kulchur*, by Gilbert Sorrentino for "the basic failure of . . . striving toward a position at which we will either forget that they are women, or, feel that they are more womanly than they are. What is usually achieved is a sort of middle-ground attitude which is neither masculine or feminine but simply, 'poetic'; as if the writing of poems is akin to a change in metabolism. This rarely occurs in poems written by men, except those poems which one may consider blatantly homosexual." The usual damned if you do and damned if you don't. Sorrentino goes on: "I don't mean to imply that all these ladies lack talent, or devotion. It is simply that the work lacks a vigor which one looks for in poetry."

*Yugen* (1958–1962), ed. by Hettie Jones. *Floating Bear* (1965–1973), ed. by Diane di Prima.

Catharine Stimpson, "The Beat Generation and the Trials of Homosexual Liberation," *Salmagundi*, 1982.

"Pull My Daisy," 1969, 29 min. Film by Robert Frank and Alfred Leslie, screenplay and narration by Jack Kerouac, music by David Amram. Distr: New Yorker Films. Starring Allen Ginsberg, Gregory Corso, Larry Rivers, David Amram, Peter Orlovsky, Alice Neel, and Delphine Seyrig in "a day in the life of the Beat Poets."

# LIVING OUR LIFE

THERE IS A CERTAIN tidal pool in the rocks on a nubble in Maine that teems with bivalves and crustaceans. For years I have gone to the pool to collect mussels, knowing I can usually find all I want there, but in all the times I've gone musseling, I have been almost unaware of the profusion of small crabs that inhabit the green sea-weed surrounding and trailing into the mussel pool. Recently when I went crabbing in the rocks and wound up at the same pool, I barely noticed the large clusters of blue mussels waiting there to be picked. This didn't surprise me; by now I've learned that when I go down to the sea on a quest with all my senses tuned I generally find what I'm looking for. Background and foreground alternate, like blue mussels and green crabs, in perfect balance with each other and with my needs.

Something similar happens when I write. Once I have settled on a subject to write about, it seems as if, almost magically, everything I see and hear bears crucially on the work I am doing. I have only to open a newspaper or turn on a radio to find half a dozen stories that seem to have been planted there like green crabs to answer my needs. Every word I hear seems relevant; every event I witness is a sign; even what is unsaid or unseen, like blue mussels on crabbing days, contributes to my work. This, I take it, is what it means to be in harmony with your environment: you look for what you can find and find what you're looking for.

So with my relation to Emma Goldman (1869–1940), the magnetic anarchist, feminist, radical activist, speaker, editor, writer, theorist, midwife, free lover, and general troublemaker, who was the subject of several of my earliest (and, as you can see, latest) writings. Although I am primarily a novelist, I have written a biography of Emma Goldman, edited two collections of her works, written essays and given talks and interviews about her, and I feel I will never tire of thinking about her. From the time I first began to study her, I have been finding in the rocky pool of her life and work precisely what I've needed to know. I, her biographer, have shaped her life, and she, my subject, has shaped mine. For better or worse, we're a couple. (Nonexclusive, naturally; she insists passionately on free love!) The major themes of my work are there in hers—or shall I say the major themes of hers are there in mine?—and it is clear to me too that in working on Emma (we have long been on a first-name basis) I developed skills, attitudes, and insights that might seem to an outsider to have little to do with hers but that I know to be inspired by hers, skills and attitudes which have been crucial in shaping my life as a writer. Not only the subject of her works and the substance of her life but also her process of self-reflection and the form of her work have affected the process and form of mine. Whether this is because I was seeking what she had to show me or because I am following a path she led me on, I can't say. Both. One.

I had been writing for about a year before I started to work on Emma in the late 1960s. When my children entered nursery school, after a lifetime of working and playing with other people's written words I began composing words of my own. Into stories, fictions. During that first year of writing I completed (but had not yet published) my first book, *Bosley on the Number Line*, a mathematical fantasy for children, and several stories for adults. Between finishing my first book, in which I had put no female characters, think-

136

ing that the adventures of a boy were much more interesting and publishable than those of a girl, and beginning my second, *To the Barricades: The Anarchist Life of Emma Goldman*, in 1967 I attended my first meeting of the young women's liberation movement. That event changed my life. From then on, the new, transforming illuminations of feminism allowed me to bring into the foreground, where I could catch them, from the background where they had lived as invisibly as crabs, ideas and events of sexual politics. Like every important work of theory or art, feminism began to make visible to me what had previously been invisible; from then on, I focused my attention on the lives, works, and history of women, and I became a fighter in our movement.

When an opportunity to write a biography of a "forgotten woman" for T. Y. Crowell's *Women of America* series was presented to me by a friend, I seized it. Here, I thought, was a chance to walk ahead on both feet of my new life: the writer (my right foot) and the feminist (my left). But that hope proved premature—it's not so easy to learn to walk. Until then, my two feet had been in unsteady alliance: instead of working smoothly together to carry me forward, sometimes they threatened to get in each other's way, causing me to falter, stumble, even trip. In the beginning phase of the women's liberation movement, there was an undercurrent of suspicion directed at writers. To many feminists, writers were seen as individualists, elitists, opportunists, ready to advance themselves by exploiting the movement, particularly if they wrote about feminism, and accusations flew. I watched and listened. I certainly didn't want to alienate my comrades or see my efforts work against the cause of feminism, to which I already owed so much, but I didn't want to stop writing either. I listened to the debate, neither accepting nor rejecting the charges.

I personally had escaped suspicion, at least temporarily, because at that time much of my work was for children, and in those days the world of children was one in which many young feminists had at best a negative interest. My writing, therefore, seemed to them unimportant. (Ironically, it was writing for children that had also enabled me, before my feminist awakening, to slip behind the lines of male literary hegemony without encountering the big guns I believed were leveled at every woman writer so arrogant as to claim authority in print. To the literary establishment, then as now, writing for children, like housework, was usually considered women's work—no challenge, no threat, hardly worth wasting ammunition on.) But the movement, ever expanding, soon raised its consciousness about writing for children: months before my first book was actually published, I and a dozen other women organized the pioneering group Feminists for Children's Media to develop a feminist critique of children's literature. Every week for many months of 1969 and 1970 we met at my apartment to examine children's books, both trade and text, until we had produced an article, a slide show, and a bibliography ("Little Miss Muffett Fights Back"), which we presented under the title "Sexism in Children's Literature" to a stunned American Library Association, to which sexism was new, as both word and concept. Subsequently, our work was taken up by many other groups and expanded to include critiques of TV, film, toys, and other media.

The Crowell *Women of America* series was ostensibly aimed at "young adults"—a step up from children, but still not elevated enough to make my work as a writer suspect, either in the movement or out. Under the double cover of *selfless work* and *insignificance* (I was helping to restore to view a "forgotten" woman whose works had long been out of print, and I was writing for the young) I hoped to walk on both feet straight into print. Far from limiting my stride as a writer, my special young audience challenged me to stretch my talents as I might not have done writing for "old" adults.

Before I began the book I made certain vows. Assuming that there is nothing young people are incapable of understanding if it is presented carefully enough, and assuming that my readers knew nothing about the history or ideas of Emma Goldman's time, I knew I had to make everything I wrote extremely clear. To be able to explain to the young such concepts as anarchism, socialism, feminism, sexual repression, revolution, as well as the complicated and exciting events of those earlier social movements, I would have to understand them so well myself as to be able to convey them with utter simplicity—a task as difficult for a writer as writing with complexity. Then, too, writing for an audience notorious for its low threshold of boredom, I decided to lure my young readers' interest by lingering over my subject's formative years. Emma's childhood in a Russian village, her response to her father's cruelty, her love of a devoted teacher, her pleasures in dancing, in reading, the first glimmerings of her intellectual and social awakenings—such experiences could do much, I thought, to make sense of a life to young readers. This decision turned out later to be invaluable to me as a novelist because it led me to search for the social and psychological roots of character. I felt that once I succeeded in capturing my readers' interest I could hold it most readily by telling my story in dramatic scenes (vowing, however, not to present a single word, feeling, or action for which there was no explicit, citable evidence)—another valuable novelistic technique. In fact, the only restriction I imposed upon myself because of my special audience was to use simple sentences instead of complex ones; but I refused to fudge any issues or rule out any subject matter, particularly the sexual, as inappropriate to youth.

With fine intentions, then, but ignorant, inexperienced, and confused, I approached Emma Goldman: ignorant about history, inexperienced as a writer, confused by the conflicting factions of the early women's liberation movement. With little confidence in my abilities and much trepidation about my ambitions as a writer, I signed a contract to write a book, determined to make my work serve, not subvert, feminism. I assembled Emma's works and began to read. And what, to my amazement, did I find? I found in Emma's words and deeds, life and times, a veritable mirror of the problems and paradoxes that we—I—in the young women's movement were wrestling with. Her concerns, conflicts, passionate struggles paralleled ours, mine. The problems of individualism, dissent, minority voice, authority, hierarchy, which were at the heart of the movement's quarrel with the world, with its own adherents, and with writers, were examined by Emma in essay after essay, event after event. Our great subjects—the relation between the sexes, the organization of society, and, most profoundly, the connection between the two—were also her great subjects. She even wrote one essay, "Intellectual Proletarians," that explicitly examined the question of the writer's relation to revolution. (Obviously, she herself was a writer whose political commitment was above suspicion.)

Not that my conclusions or my emphases were the same as hers: I did not even consider myself an anarchist. But of what teacher and student is identity ever required? A good teacher helps you develop in your own direction, helps make you aware of the variety of life in the tidal pools for you to harvest as you choose. Our differences, our many quarrels, were quite as instructive as our agreements, since they focused on the same crucial questions to which our separate times, lives, and ways had, astonishingly, led us. Her times became my school, her books my text and commentaries, just as, in the progress of my book, retrospectively mine became hers.

Thinking about Emma's ideas forced me to deepen and expand my own. And she, who lived her packed life at the center of the great political and social upheavals of her time, recognizing the patriarchal family, capitalism, and the state as equal united forces against liberty, she gave me a greatly expanded context in which to analyze the gender relations around which my social awareness had flowered. In the women's liberation movement I had discovered how the personal was not petty but political; from Emma, who tried always to live by her principles, I learned how the seemingly great, the "political," was personal. She embraced with the passion of principle such concerns and activities as free love, midwifery, contraception, children's schools, literature, and magazine editing with no less ardor than she brought to her participation in the Russian Revolution and the Spanish Civil War. When I reflected on her life, a life in which selfless participation was indistinguishable from self-assertion and fulfillment, a life so much longer and larger than mine, I began to understand the connections between authority and oppression, individual and society, anarchism and feminism, sex and politics—the very connections our movement was struggling with and I had discovered were so necessary to social understanding. By leading me to explore relations I had not previously thought to explore, Emma led me to a method of analysis that gave me the confidence and therefore the courage to write with conviction. And the method was this: Through anarchist doctrine and its practice in Emma's life, I learned to question authority, all authority, including the movement's. Soon I realized that despite the movement's suspicions, not only was there no conflict between the writer and the feminist in me (I was in fact a feminist writing), but there was nothing I could not study and think about deeply enough to write about if I chose. In this way, she led me into the world.

And not only through her ideas. Through her actions too. By example, she taught me to trust my ideas and to act with courage. In her life she was frequently considered a pariah. She was arrested countless times, shunned, persecuted, chased from country to country. (She was proud to be the first political deportee from the United States.) Yet her resolute rejection of authority, which left her with only her integrity and her own ideas, feelings, and principles to rely upon, turned each persecution into a kind of strength. "The more opposition I encountered," she crowed, "the more I was in my element." With Emma constantly demonstrating to me that courage strengthens, at least when it is cushioned by a movement, how could I continue to coddle my own small terrors? I had to fight them. The first time I faced a furious crowd at a political demonstration, the first time I defied a police order, the first time I published an article under my own name instead of a pseudonym, the first time I triumphantly overcame my shyness and insecurity and dared to speak before an audience or teach a class, I felt the encouraging hand and smiling nod of Emma behind me.

In this way, Emma's essays and exploits formed, as it were, my lesson plans. But I also discovered in her work more esoteric lessons, not only of content but of form, lessons important to my development as a writer. In addition to her essays, speeches, books on political and social subjects, Emma wrote a long, detailed first-person account of her own life, rich in personal interpretation and speculation, her 1,000-page autobiography, *Living My Life*. Reading this astonishing specimen of biography when I was about to write a biography myself was like discovering crabs at the mussel pool. Although I must surely have read many other biographies and autobiographies before *Living My Life*, Emma's was the first one I remember reading with a writer's eye, as much aware of the writer as of the subject of the book. Until then I hadn't needed such dual awareness.

Here I must say that ever since I began writing I have been unable to read "innocently"; I approach most of what I read as a writer primarily observing another writer's techniques for conveying the subtleties of meaning. I read most self-consciously when the book is fiction, since I write mostly fiction. I can no longer lose myself in a novel and can lose myself in a work of nonfiction only when it is in a form or on a subject I don't usually tackle in my own work.

For my new work I needed to know how to interpret a life. How did one begin to reflect upon the fluid multiplicity of experiences that comprise a life? I was puzzled less about how to discover what happened than about what the happenings meant; how could one draw conclusions about the motives, actions, intentions behind events, even supposing one knew the events? Just as I sank myself into these questions, I read *Living My Life*, and there was Emma freely demonstrating before my eyes one way to do it, teaching me how to squeeze the meaning from the events of a life. Taking as her subject a life she knew well, her own, she unabashedly used her own clear, all-embracing vision, her anarchism, to guide her through the swarming events of her life and help her decide which events were most significant, which required reflection, how to interpret for herself and her readers her experience. Reading her life, I not only glimpsed her living it, but I saw her mind and character at work writing it. And I saw that my own vision might be able to guide me through a different set of events.

Even without corroborating her reports of events from other sources (a task on which, eventually, I spent most of my research time), I discovered that I had to read Emma on two levels at once, observing what she revealed consciously and what unconsciously. Sometimes her reports were convincing, sometimes suspect; here she seemed self-serving, there cautious, elsewhere over-generous or defensive or mean. Like all of us, she championed her version of the "facts" and let her passion and temperament color her judgment. (The summary running heads at the top of each page of *Living My Life* are themselves as revealing as they are entertaining. A brief sampling: *I enthrall my audiences / I speak on patriotism / Ben satisfies my deepest yearning; Donald betrays our comrades / I disseminate birth-control propaganda / I am arrested / Billy Sunday nauseates me / I help sexual unfortunates / we triumph in San Diego / I talk atheism to theologians / I begin to grow weary of Ben / I relax at Provincetown / the benefits of reading / the Fourth of July in prison / the liberals disgust me / I disagree with Frank Harris / Ben and I break for good.*) But her unconscious disclosures were no less expressions of character than were her explicit boasts and confessions. The interplay of hidden influence, chance event, intention, opportunity, desire, which together with the whole of history make up character, paraded past as Emma consciously and unconsciously revealed her life.

Now, portraying or revealing character through event is precisely what a novelist does too. Studying Emma's autobiography, I incidentally learned what it means to present a life in the first person, with all the powers and limitations of that point of view. And as I tried to understand her life "objectively," I found myself relying on what is ultimately, after all the research has been done, the novelist's chief method for creating character: introspection. You enter into the life of your subject, your character, by *becoming* your character. You put yourself in the precise situation your character is in and observe your own reactions and feelings. To be able to do this, naturally you must know every possible detail of the situation, large and small, distant and close, hidden and apparent; you must master all the facts you can of your character's time, place, heredity, environment. But this process only facilitates the final step: to know your subject from inside, through an act of empathy, of introspection. Perhaps because *Living My Life* was written by a woman whose concerns so closely paralleled mine, I found myself putting myself into her situation with relative ease. Naturally, I read everything I could about her and her times; but before I could begin to write about Emma with any confidence, I had to develop what I later discovered to be my main method of writing fiction, a method that might for all I know horrify most historians: checking my subject's feelings against my own.

Of course, writing a nonfiction life, a biography, demands a different relation to the names and "facts" than fiction requires. Different conventions govern, different rules must be followed. Whereas in fiction you try to imagine an event to convey your meaning, in biography you usually try to imagine a meaning to illuminate an event. But biography and autobiography are no less fictions than novels are. Character must be imagined, significance imposed, events interpreted, and from a flowing stream of moments some must be diverted by the writer to cut a new bed.

Emma's was the first life aside from my own that I undertook to interpret. It was an all but forbidding task, so formidable that I found the restrictions imposed by the rules of biography reassuring and even comforting. Since the form of my book was, in a sense, given, I felt as if I were taking a limited risk as a writer. It was not only the genre, with its givens, that made me feel relatively secure; I felt Emma there ready to talk over with me every problem, every idea. As it was her life I was writing, not mine, she shared my risk: Every tentative statement I made, I could support with a quote from her. Under her guidance, with her own story as model and inspiration, I was able to exercise my powers of reflection, interpretation, and imagination one muscle at a time, without the risk of collapsing, until eventually I was ready to throw off the bonds of biography, loose my imagination, follow my bent, and undertake to write a novel. A year after I finished *To the Barricades* I felt I had sufficiently mastered the process of introspection and interpretation—in other words, I had learned enough empathy and confidence—not only to walk on my two feet but to march, to dance.

And I had learned how to give shape to a life. Beginning, middle, climax, end. Intimation, development, resolution. The elusive working out of a destiny. It was no accident that my first two novels were cast in the form of fictional autobiographies: first-person fictions, each telling the life of a single central character. I had learned to reflect on a life in the workshop of Emma Goldman.

When I finished *To the Barricades* and was selecting my next subject, I briefly considered writing a biography of Emma's longtime lover and business manager, Dr. Ben Reitman. A complicated and colorful character, once elected King of the Hobos, he was criticized by Emma's friends as politically suspect and rejected by them as unworthy of her. Like Emma, I found him fascinating and sexy; besides, I was still caught up in Emma's life and wanted to champion her right to choose her own lovers. (There were too many people in our movement who wanted to dictate to others the correct way to live, and I wanted to present them with Emma's defiant response: "Censorship from comrades had the same effect on me as police persecution; it made me surer of myself.") But the year was 1969. A great new audience of women hungry to know about women was gathering. Many of us in the movement believed that it would be a diversion from our urgent cause to devote our major energies to men when so many remarkable women were unknown and needed to be heard about. I could not in conscience choose a man for my next subject. Emma had had a hand in rescuing me from what seemed like a dangerously passive life; the least I could do was carry on the rescue operation. Following Emma's lead, I undertook to edit a collection of Emma's speeches and essays, some of which I had found in manuscript and discovered had never before been published, others of which had not been published since Emma published them herself in her magazine *Mother Earth* early in the century. By making these works available in my collection *Red Emma Speaks* (Random House, 1972), I hoped that others might get the same boost from reading Emma that her work had given me; I also hoped to repay some of the debt I owed her for lending me her life as a subject and for helping my career. (She of course would scoff at the idea of a debt; as an anarchist, she thought ideas and assistance ought to be free to anyone who could use them and never even bothered to copyright *Mother Earth*.) And when that book was done, I decided to drop the shield of the past and the protective distance granted an editor and a biographer and to write what I most wanted to write: a novel, set in the present, about ourselves.

My first adult novel, *Memoirs of an Ex-Prom Queen* (Knopf, 1972), is the story of Sasha Davis, a private middle-class Midwestern girl with no political awareness at all, whose main concerns are beauty and boys. As such it may seem very far from the history Emma presents of a born Russian rebel who spends her life all over the Western world publicly promoting reform and revolution. Mine is a comic novel; Emma's story is earnest and energetically pedagogical. Perhaps no one but the authors could see the connection. Yet I know that the underlying impulse behind the book, to show the way ideology and social forces become a kind of destiny for the heroine, was inspired by Emma.

From the time Sasha enters kindergarten until she is ready to pack up her children and leave her second husband, she thinks that if she is everything her society expects her to be she can somehow escape her destiny. We see her as a prude and a sexpot; dumb and cunning; beautiful, popular prom queen, devoted wife and mother. But of course, Sasha always winds up facing another impossible bind.

Emma might well miss the essential irony of my novel and be impatient with my Sasha, hopelessly unconscious and middle class;

patience was never one of Emma's virtues. Nevertheless, as a tribute to her inspiration and for the authority her words confer on my subject, I opened my novel about the adventures of a high school beauty queen with the following epigraph from Emma's *Living My Life*:

> On the Sunday of my first lecture a sealed note was left at my hotel for me. The anonymous writer warned me of a plot against my life: I was going to be shot when about to enter the hall, he assured me. . . . I walked leisurely from the hotel to the meeting-place. When within half a block of it I instinctively raised to my face the large bag I always carried. I got safely into the hall and walked towards the platform still holding the bag in front of my face. All through the lecture the thought persisted in my brain: "If I could only protect my face!" Surely no man would think of his face under such circumstances. Yet I, in the presence of probable death, had been afraid to have my face disfigured! It was a shock to discover in myself such ordinary female vanity.

Yes, even in Emma Goldman!

My second novel, *Burning Questions* (Knopf, 1978), bears a much more obvious connection to Emma's work. This book, I like to think, Emma would have approved of and enjoyed. Another first-person "memoir," the story of the evolution of a contemporary radical feminist, the novel almost parodies the genre Emma wrote in, the revolutionary memoir. Starting with Emma's own, I searched out and studied all the autobiographies of revolutionary women I could find, from the pre-Russian Revolutionary martyrs to such American radicals as Mother Jones, Mother Bloor, and Elizabeth Gurley Flynn, in order to distill the elements common to them all for the "autobiography" of my heroine, Zane IndiAnna.

Zane comes from a small Midwestern town in a time when, as she says in her own preface, "my generation seemed to consist of nothing but jocks, grinds, and the contented"—worlds and aeons away from the seething childhoods of most of her revolutionary predecessors. Unlike the nonfictional revolutionary memoirs I studied, in which irony seems to be all but impermissible, my book is filled with irony. Still, the form of Zane's memoir, the transforming events she recalls of her youth, the details she chooses to emphasize, the shape of her life, and the very title of her book (*My Life as a Rebel*) closely parallel those of her models. Like them, Zane leaves home seeking adventure and a life of significance, follows her passions, gives herself to her movement, proudly recounts her running battle with the police (Zane gleefully presents her readers with her own FBI dossier), and even manages to find good sex. She carries on a running dialogue with her heroes, including, of course, Emma, and there on the reading list with which Zane naturally ends her own book is—what else?—*Living My Life*.

Even my third novel, *On the Stroll* (Knopf, 1981), though written in the third person rather than the first and begun a full decade after I began writing about Emma, owes a good deal to Emma. *To the Barricades* was, after all, written in the third person; writing that book I had to learn to become a narrator with a point of view separate from that of my subjects and characters and to write with authority different from that of my sources. The story of a teenage prostitute named Robin, a shopping-bag lady named Owl, and a pimp named Prince, *On the Stroll* draws on Emma's concern with society's outcasts in more ways than I can name. From the time I first read Emma's essay on prostitution, "The Traffic in Women" (which I included in both of my anthologies and, as part of a feminist action, read into the record of a New York City legislative hearing on "victimless" crimes), I wanted to write about a prostitute. And Ben Reitman's only published book, *The Second Oldest Profession*, published by Emma's Mother Earth Publishing Company, a pioneering if quirky study of pimps (whom he served as physician), sparked my early fascination with the relationship between prostitutes and pimps. At least as far back as the 1969 New York Radical Feminist Prostitution Conference, prostitution and sex were issues that divided the women's movement, even as they had in Emma's day. Like Emma, I always found the puritan strain within our movement, which surfaced at that conference, as distressing as puritanism without. (I left that organization after the Conference.) Although my interest never led me to try to turn tricks as Emma did on one occasion (if there's one thing she can't stand it's a competitive attitude among comrades), I did want to take a stand, as Emma had.

One night in the mid-1970s, something happened that convinced me to write my own book about a prostitute. When the Democratic National Convention came to New York City, the mayor ordered the police to get the prostitutes off the streets. A group of feminists organized by feminist lawyer Flo Kennedy decided to fight such police harassment of women by taking up positions on the street corners of the Stroll (the part of the city where the prostitutes walk), warning the police that if they arrested any women for just standing around, they'd be charged with false arrest. I joined the group. And a strange thing happened to me that night. As I stood around on the Stroll, the people who until then had usually inspired fear in me, like the men who hang out in the streets, suddenly became my allies; and those whom I didn't ordinarily fear, like the police and the men in business suits (the prostitutes' main potential customers), began to appear threatening. I resolved then to try to convey this illuminating experience to others and understood that to do so I would have to explore this life from the inside—a vantage point I might never have dared without Emma there before me.

Not only Robin the prostitute and Prince the pimp but my bag lady too derives partly from my work on Emma. Though Owl doesn't know it herself, never having had much interest in politics, she has Emma Goldman's physique, tenacity, spectacles, and something more.

Would I have learned similar lessons about the shape of a life and about narrative approaches if I had written a biography of someone else? Probably. When I go looking for crabs, even in the mussel pool, I find crabs. And I might have learned introspective empathy and gained the necessary confidence to write about someone else, since these were the skills I needed at the time. As I said, by the time I discovered Emma I had already begun to question authority: I'd been writing for a year and had been startled awake by the new feminist movement. But if I had signed a contract to write about someone whose puzzles and passions less clearly mirrored my own, it might have been harder for me to cultivate the habit of empathy; and if my subject had been less egalitarian and libertarian, less feminist and questioning than Emma, or if my first subject had happened to be a man, I'm not sure I would have gained the confidence I needed to risk exposure in print.

Let's say I was lucky in choosing Emma as my first subject, not least because I was able to see confirmed in her life what I had already begun to know in my own: that an idea, a cause, a movement could give meaning to a life. Maybe I would have learned different lessons with a different teacher, maybe not. I don't know. I can't say I'm dissatisfied.

One could do worse than have Emma as a guide to how to end life as well as how to live it. "My fiftieth birthday I spent in the Missouri penitentiary. What more fitting place for the rebel to celebrate such an occasion? Fifty years! I felt as if I had five hundred on my back, so replete with events had been my life." Shortly after that birthday, she was deported from the United States to the Soviet Union, where she launched a new round of dissent. In the next decades she wrote her memoirs in France, fought fascism in Spain, and in Canada at the age of sixty-five had a love affair with a man of thirty-six with whom she found "complete harmony in ideas . . . and complete fulfillment of my woman soul." Until the day she died, at seventy, she kept on fighting, questioning, loving.

Can it be that once again Emma seems to know just what I need to learn? Or is it rather that I want to learn what she has to teach? I'm afraid after a couple has been together as long as we have such questions become impossible to answer.

# DANCES WITH FEMINISTS

"IF I CAN'T DANCE I DON'T want to be in your revolution," said
Emma Goldman (1869–1940), feminist hero, anarchist agitator, and
prolific writer.

Or did she? Perhaps she said, "If I can't dance I don't want to be
*part of* your revolution," as my purple T-shirt claims under a picture
of Emma looking demure in a wide-brimmed hat. Or was it rather,
"If I can't dance *to it, it's not my* revolution," as the quote appears in
a 1983 "non-sexist yet traditional" Passover Haggadah?

In fact, though the sentiment is indeed Emma Goldman's, one
she frequently pronounced and acted upon, she wrote none of the
above, notwithstanding that each of these versions and more has
been attributed to her on buttons, posters, banners, T-shirts, bum-
per stickers, and in books and articles, for decades. Here, rather, is
what she did say, in her 1931 autobiography *Living My Life*:

> At the dances I was one of the most untiring and gayest. One eve-
> ning a cousin of Sasha [Alexander Berkman], a young boy, took me
> aside. With a grave face, as if he were about to announce the death
> of a dear comrade, he whispered to me that it did not behoove an
> agitator to dance. Certainly not with such reckless abandon, any-

*way. It was undignified for one who was on the way to become a force in the anarchist movement. My frivolity would only hurt the Cause.*

*I grew furious at the impudent interference of the boy. I told him to mind his own business, I was tired of having the Cause constantly thrown into my face. I did not believe that a Cause which stood for a beautiful ideal, for anarchism, for release and freedom from conventions and prejudice, should demand the denial of life and joy. I insisted that our Cause could not expect me to become a nun and that the movement should not be turned into a cloister. If it meant that, I did not want it. "I want freedom, the right to self-expression, everybody's right to beautiful, radiant things." Anarchism meant that to me, and I would live it in spite of the whole world—prisons, persecution, everything. Yes, even in spite of the condemnation of my own closest comrades I would live my beautiful ideal.*

As I may, inadvertently and indirectly, bear some responsibility for the extrapolation from authentic text to familiar paraphrase, I would like to confess and set the record straight. Here is what happened. Sometime early in 1973 I received a phone call from one Jack Frager, an old-time anarchist who worked in the anarchist center at 339 Lafayette Street in Lower Manhattan—a building where to this day various radical groups, including anarchists and the War Resisters League, have their offices. Like many dedicated radicals of the era before desktop publishing, he was a printer; now he had the original idea to raise funds for the Cause by printing up a batch of Emma Goldman T-shirts to hawk in Central Park at the huge upcoming festival celebrating the end of the Vietnam War. Having heard me lecture to the anarchists on Emma's feminism (after decades of obscurity during which all of her works were out of print, Emma was suddenly returning to the public eye as a hero of women's liberation), Jack was phoning to solicit my help.

I had recently published two books on Emma: a biography and a collection of her essays, both of which contained photos of her. He wondered if I might lend him a glossy photo from which to print, and also asked me to suggest a phrase or slogan from Emma's writings suitable for emblazoning on T-shirts.

Delighted by the opportunity to publicize Emma's feminist side, particularly among followers sometimes reluctant to share her with any movement not strictly anarchist, I offered him a glossy head shot of a stalwart, hatless Emma in pince-nez and referred him to several prose passages, particularly the dancing episode, which seemed to me to embody her most lively feminist spirit. Did I propose Emma's statement about "freedom, the right to self-expression, everybody's right to beautiful, radiant things"? Perhaps. In gratitude, Jack promised me all the T-shirts I wanted, at cost.

Several days later, when I picked up my shirts along with my precious glossy, I was surprised to find a succinct abridgement of Emma's dance story spread boldly across the shirt—the First (and most common) version of the now-famous slogan: "If I can't dance I don't want to be in your revolution."

I searched Emma's texts for the statement; it was nowhere to be found. But Jack was so pleased, the festival was so soon, Emma looked so lively printed in red and black on a variety of rich background colors, that I hadn't the heart to register an objection in the name of scholarship. After all, the apocrypha appeared on a mere gross or two of T-shirts, which surely could not require the same standards of accuracy as, say, book blurbs extracted from book reviews—and the sentiment expressed was pure Emma indeed. But history (and fashion) exploded so quickly in those hungrily feminist days that the slogan on the original shirt-run was soon dispersed and copied and broadcast nationwide and abroad, underground and above, sometimes, absent a text to be checked against, changing along the way like a child's game of Telephone, until Jack's initial light-hearted liberties had taken wing as quotable lore and soared up into the realms of myth.

When all my shirts from the original batch had been given away to friends and my own worn to a rag, I decided to buy another. Only the new shirt, purchased in an uptown bookstore, sported a different picture of Emma—this time in a floppy hat—and a different version of the by now legendary legend, different still from the one I sometimes flaunt on a button. But, hey, if you can't wear what you like, who wants to be in your revolution?

# LATE LIFE

# THOUGHTS AT SEVENTY

IS SEVENTY OLD? I used to think so, but now I'm not sure. Age is so confusing. Despairingly I described myself at twenty-five as "a quarter-century old," while the gravity of turning fifty compelled me to reinvigorate my life, then write a book about it. Except chronologically, "old," whether in the negative sense of obsolescent or the positive sense of experienced, is an ever-moving target.

Emma Goldman died at seventy and claimed to have had her most fulfilling love affair at sixty-five. When I was in my thirties writing a biography of her, I thought that seventy was not too young to die and sixty-five was rather old to have great sex. Now I think neither. At seventy, with my health still good, partner holding up, work in progress, political action urgent, seventy doesn't feel particularly old to me. But it depends on who's asking.

A new friend, a poet not yet fifty, with whom I've been drinking mango margaritas in an East Village bar, greets my announcement of my age with stunned disbelief, surprised to learn that she has been trading secrets with a *seventy-year-old*. It's obvious that to her seventy is ancient. I could be her mother. But another friend, in her sixties, directs her surprise at my very question. "You're not old in any bad sense," she says indignantly, adding that if I think

157

so I've been bamboozled, because our ideas about age are socially constructed.

I know she's right. Otherwise the respect and stature we sometimes accord to age would graph consistently, and not, as now, slope up for some cultures, professions, people, slope down for others, and look like a dizzying roller coaster for still others.

Compared to the heavy burden of age I felt in my early thirties—panicked over the impending loss of youth about to finish me off—seventy feels positively young. Remember the 1960s slogan, "don't trust anyone over thirty"? Remember the thirty-year-old admission age to Older Women's Liberation (OWL)? Never have I felt older or more irrelevant than before feminism's Second Wave, when thirty was considered over-the-hill (for women) and the last safe age to begin a family, and your life was supposed to be fulfilled by having babies. Still feeling then like a 1950s middle class Midwestern girl, though living in New York, I retired from full-time work to become a mother; and by the time my youngest started school I was a disillusioned wife with a wandering husband, no savings, no prospects, no future. A has-been at thirty-four!

Then the women's liberation movement hit New York and quickly restored my youthful ardor. Suddenly I had a compelling purpose and important work. Far from being a has-been, I knew life had not, would not pass me by. Fired by movement passion, in quick succession I defied my husband, began organizing women's groups, gave my first speech, wrote my first essay and before long my first novel. Though that early movement euphoria couldn't last, I never again felt as impotent or "old" as I had before it touched me. In an instant I switched from a woman with a past ("old") to one with a future ("young").

It's possible that everything could as suddenly change again. A critical fall, a devastating death, dementia, the bomb, an economic crash could conceivably age me as rapidly as the women's movement made me young. But hair has been known to whiten overnight at twenty; disaster can strike at any age, and some disasters feel like opportunities. It's not age that could befall me but despair.

Still, some sobering changes I've experienced lately do derive from my age—not least, my steady awareness that my end is in sight. But other, derivative changes have an opposite effect, less sobering than elating. At seventy, many pressures I used to suffer are falling away. No more (anyway, far less) driving ambition, relentlessly prospective thinking, unrealistic expectations, Utopian delusions—those anxieties of youth and middle age that keep people strained and guilty. At fifty, to ease those concerns and free myself from others' judgments, I took myself off to an island where, living in complete solitude, I could do whatever I liked instead of what was expected of me. At seventy, knowing what I know, such anxieties seem so pointless that I am able to enjoy some of the freedoms I discovered on that remote island smack in the middle of New York City. On impulse, last weekend I spent an entire day strolling through the zoo without a hint of guilt. This extra measure of freedom makes me feel, paradoxically, "young,"—if young means, as cliché would have it, carefree.

Not that I'm immune to the weight of mere chronology. I admit I've often considered "old" those of my friends who are older than I by a decade or more, no matter how like-minded or free-spirited. Now I laugh at myself to remember that when I was forty and met my closest friend, then fifty-three, I marveled that a woman of her age and generation could feel exactly as I did about so many things. (She also knew a lot I didn't.) When she turned sixty-five (then seventy, eighty, now eighty-three), my celebratory wonder remained, as constant as the difference between our ages. Even now, with her bones and memory getting thin, her savvy continues to amaze me. On the other hand, I'm less aware of my age difference with my younger friends (except for one, whose deference drives it home). To me we're all just—well—friends, though *they* may secretly feel otherwise.

One's age sense is inextricable from the shared culture and experience of one's generation, time, and place. Veterans of movements or wars, of shared traumas or triumphs, often feel an ineffable, exclusive affinity. It's the rare imagination that can permanently switch generations. Last night, seeing two movies from the 1940s on cable, I was unexpectedly reminded of how long I've been around, how much I've lived. The matchless movie stars of my childhood—Hedy Lamarr, Rita Hayworth, Joan Crawford, Greta Garbo, Mae West—who once defined for me beauty, glamour, style—can't have the same meaning for later generations. In the back room of my consciousness they remain the ideal. Subsequent stars never seemed the real thing; I never pored over *their* pictures in magazines. Instead I grew up. After I had children I got so caught up in movement politics and motherhood that I was way too busy to go to the movies. When, after missing two decades' worth of films, I finally gazed up at the screen again, I didn't recognize the stars. Who were those newcomers and upstarts? Accomplished actors they might be—but not stars, as my cohort conceived them.

I left high school in 1950. My music is pre-rock. My defining war was World War II. My battle for justice began with civil rights. My children have reached their midlife. My parents are dead. My partner naps in the afternoon. Suddenly seeing the old stars vamp across the light years back into my life, I realize with a certain pleasure and even pride that, given the human lifespan, seventy may indeed be getting old.

# SUMMER JEW

HOW STARTLING TO DISCOVER IN my maturity an affinity with my grandfather the scrap-metal peddler. From the first decade of the twentieth century until after World War II, first in a horse-drawn cart, then in a truck, he scoured rural Pennsylvania and eastern Ohio for abandoned machinery, cars, stoves, tools, pots and pans, which he sold by the ton whenever he amassed enough to fill a railway freight car. Though he wore no beard or yarmulke, I wonder what the Midwestern Christian burghers and farmers whom he solicited thought of him, a Jew with a heavy Yiddish accent who could lift the front of a car off the ground with his bare hands.

Part of a minuscule Jewish minority when not the only Jewish family in town, my grandparents kept moving until, following my mother's birth in a Pennsylvania hamlet, the youngest of seven children, they moved permanently to a large Jewish community in Cleveland, Ohio, where they finally felt at home. There my mother was educated and assimilated, married a Jewish atheist attorney, and conceived me. I grew up before and during World War II in a middle-class Cleveland suburb among Jews and Christians living together in easy truce. Which meant that in our high school of roughly half Jews, half Christians, we never mixed socially but did

ALIX KATES SHULMAN

acknowledge each other's capabilities and prowess. Everyone knew exactly who was which, and since our rigid system of social clubs kept us with our own, we all took our ethnicity for granted. So confident was I of fitting into my limited realm that I had no notion of what it meant to belong to a small minority in the larger world.

Nor did my move at twenty from our Cleveland suburb to New York City, with its vibrant Jewish culture, enlighten me: if I was an embarrassed outsider attempting to disguise my origins it was not because I was Jewish but because I was Midwestern (the twang, the smiles, the clothes). Indeed, as an atheist in a cosmopolitan world, I was so unconcerned about Jewish identity that in my ten-member New York radical feminist women's group, which met weekly for a decade to discuss the most intimate details of our lives, I was oblivious of who was or wasn't Jewish until the day we decided to discuss Ethnicity.

So it came as a shock, after my husband built us a seaside cabin on a small coastal island in Maine, to find myself sporting Jewish identity like a red banner. Not that anyone ever so much as alluded to our ethnicity in my presence (although over the years, on the ferry between Portland and the islands, I did hear several drunken anti-Semitic tirades directed to no one in particular). But after decades of my Jewish identity being obscured in the blur of Jews around me, I suddenly felt as if I were outlined in felt-tipped pen: Jew.

To start with, there was our Jewish name: Shulman (which some islanders had a hard time pronouncing: Shuman? Sherman?). And if that didn't label us, my husband's college classmate, a teacher who had lured us to the island in the first place and was a permanent, church-going member of that small, mostly fishing community of a hundred-odd households, let it be known. Perhaps as the only Jewish family in town we were an exotic feather in his cap, who could tell? In any case, whether feather, foreigner, or foe, the feeling was novel to me, and from then on I was seldom unaware of our family's singularity.

We had bought our property from a previous island Jew, a man named Bernstein, who had spent time there briefly, between 1939, when he acquired some land and built himself a small cottage, and 1941, when he sold his entire property, except for the piece we bought from him in the 1960s. When I reconnected with him recently in Portland, I asked him if he had experienced anti-Semitism on the island. He told me, "I only ever heard one remark: 'The Jews are buying up the whole island.'" At 88 his memory was sharp, and he reminded me that there had once been another island Jew who had a cottage in the woods, a poet who was the son of the well-known novelist Ludwig Lewisohn. But the poet committed some violent crime, and after he was sent to prison there were no more Jews on the island until we arrived in the mid-1960s.

Awkwardly I filled the niche of representative Jew. Every time we boarded the ferry I shushed my exuberant children, forbidding them to run around the deck like other children. To my surprise, when I spoke, a honeyed, ladylike trill replaced my normally raunchy speech. During our brief stays at our cabin, which in those days totaled a couple of weeks a summer, I greeted strangers on the beach with smiles and twitters—partly as disguise but also partly as insurance against anonymous assault. Not that I thought the occasional winter vandals of our cabin anti-Semites; more likely they were anti-summer-folk or unconscious teenagers on a binge. But I couldn't be sure, and why risk giving offense? In our cabin at the far end of South Beach on an isolated point without electricity, phone, road, or nearby neighbor, I felt us vulnerable.

When our buxom Boston friend Barbara, who often stayed in our cabin in our absence, was daily sighted skinny-dipping off our rocks by old Everett Clark, the storekeeper, who sat in his car tracking her through binoculars, I was glad that at least she wasn't Jewish.

That was in the 1960s and 1970s, when we used our cabin only for the occasional weeklong vacation, and there was no call to fit in. Then, in the 1980s, with the children grown, everything changed for me. Divorced and free, I began to live alone on the island from late June to early October year after year, writing, thinking, subsisting on the shellfish and wild greens I collected, studying the natural surround, becoming part of the landscape.

Not, however, part of the community. Perhaps if I'd made some friends I would have felt like a particular person rather than the summer Jew. But relishing my newfound solitude and the freedom that accompanied my social and geographical isolation, I remained aloof from all but a few people. If the price of being reclusive was to be stereotyped, I didn't care. Conscious of my various identities only in the presence of others, as a loner I was usually oblivious of my Jewish origins—as I was of my gender, my age, my class, my appearance. Alone, I was simply myself—that supreme delight of the solitary life.

Then in 1995 I published a memoir about my low-tech island life, *Drinking the Rain*, which overnight transformed my island status. Not only did it blow my anonymity, rendering my disguises useless, but the quirky loner living out on a distant point emerged as a minor local celebrity, honored at mainland bookstore chains, interviewed on TV. I became transparent to all who read my book, and it seemed that everyone on South Beach that summer was reading it; island reading groups discussed it; the island library sponsored public readings from it; the local B&B and the gift shop each offered it for sale. Embraced by the community, I felt for the first time accepted, protected, even welcome—no longer simply the Jew.

Now fast forward to the end of the millennium. The boom of the 1990s has brought development to our island. Old houses have changed hands; new houses have been constructed; people from ever farther away are buying in; the store has replaced its dried beans and grains with good cheeses and fine wines. When my nearest neighbors, directly across South Beach from me, a courtly couple from Montreal, died of old age, their house was bought by, of all people, a couple from New York, one of them a Jew whom I had vaguely known on the left in the 1960s and who knew many of my friends. Stunned (I can still hardly believe it!), I felt my two long-divergent lives, summer and winter, begin to converge. That same year, just up the road from them a New Hampshire couple, the wife Jewish, built a house from scratch. And I learned that another New York couple, retired musicians, at least one of them Jewish, had moved onto the other side of the island. All at once our small island hosted four Jewish households, three of them from New York, three of them clustered around South Beach in what I jokingly call our accidental ghetto.

Like the U.S. Supreme Court when it took on women, the island feels transformed and my own life basically, perhaps irrevocably, altered. After two decades of living in satisfying isolation, I have found in my nearest neighbors a pair of buddies, soul mates even, who recognize and know me for who I am—which includes being an atheistic, secular Jew for whom being Jewish is little more than an afterthought. When they are in residence we often laugh and eat together, spilling the stories of our lives. I believe it's our common values, politics, and history far more than our Jewish bond that enables me to let down my guard with them and merge my winter and summer selves. Not that I didn't initially resist the demise of my reclusive self-image in face of their camaraderie. But quickly the sweet delights of friendship, of knowing and being known, seduced me.

I was particularly glad to have that friendship during a recent encounter which confirmed that at least to some I was still The Jew, despite the island's new acceptance of me.

I was at the island library autographing copies of my newest book for a library benefit when I noticed with interest a stack of booklets written by another islander—a compilation of biblical proverbs in modern translation arranged by topic (nagging wife, evil men, happiness, sadness, sinning, prostitutes, holding your tongue, etc.). The following day I received in the mail a gift of a Bible, Old and New Testaments, in the same modern translation, inscribed to me by the librarian, "This living translation of God's word, may it come alive to you." Was it offered in response to my interest in the proverbs book? I received it gratefully, with only a whisper of worry, until the next day, when the author of the proverbs compilation walked across South Beach to my cabin to hand me a copy of her book, saying, "The Lord sent me to you."

If only I had thought to say, as did my Jewish neighbor after I reported the episode to him, "Well, He gave you the wrong address." More likely it was the librarian who had sent her. When my visitor urged me to come to church on Sunday to hear her deliver a sermon, I felt under attack. I've had many things in my long life, but one I expect never to get is religion. Suddenly I was all Jew, proclaiming my heritage in my defense (as if she didn't know it!).

"Our Lord was also a Jew," she shot back.

It was probably overreaction that led me to announce with mounting vehemence that while prizing my Jewish culture and tradition, I was an ardent atheist, like my father before me, which precluded my attending church except for weddings and funerals. Furthermore, I declared, in an effort to quash her designs on me, as firmly as she believed in her religion, I embraced my atheism, having held it for all of my sixty-seven years.

Undaunted, she replied, "It took me forty-nine years before I heard the Word." And opening her substantial arms she hugged me long and hard.

I took stock. What was happening? Was this biblical double whammy a colonizing response to the recent 400 percent increase in the island's Jewish population—a hostile takeover? Or was it, as was more likely, a kindly (or as she might say, loving, or better yet, Christian) gesture of salvation toward a fellow islander who through my writing had become newly accessible? If the latter, then in place of my fierce defense I should merely have thanked her with a smile and politely declined the invitation.

When I read in a local paper the headline, "Baptists' Conversion Campaign Irks Jews," I was relieved and amused. The article reported that the Southern Baptist International Mission Board had distributed a new pocket prayer guide to its 40,000 churches to coincide with the Jewish holidays, offering *tips on how to evangelize Jews during their ten holy days, when they are sensitized to spiritual matters. "Pray each day for Jewish individuals you know by name," it suggests. . . . The book suggests that after the shofar is blown on Rosh Hashanah, "many Jews will be asked to remember Abraham's call to sacrifice his son, Isaac. Ask God to reveal the truth of his own Fatherly sacrifice." The book urges Christians to pray on day eight of the High Holy Days that "Jewish people would be free of the strong influence of materialism" and implies that most Jews are atheist.*

Then it wasn't me. It was all of us. I was one of thousands, perhaps tens of thousands, who received those prayers. I was in my element.

On the island, however, my element is very small. That I have someone to laugh with over the incident makes me feel stronger and more secure than when I was the only Jew. But at the same time, the incident has left me feeling more The Jew than ever. Is it because the word Jew has at last been spoken? Or does it finally come down to a matter of numbers, as my grandparents thought? As one of several Jews on the island, I no longer feel I shoulder the entire burden of representing Jewish identity; but that doesn't bring me any closer to my winter feeling of being so comfortably lost in my Jewishness that I can take it for granted. In retrospect I find it ironic that of my several self-defining tags, from radical feminist to author of sexually explicit novels to political activist, any of which might be expected to raise an island eyebrow, the one label I feel gleaming on my island breast is Jew. Why? Is it because *Jew* is a ready-made identity about which everyone, including myself, has an opinion—or because I am in a tiny minority? How else explain that I, who have been coming to this island for nearly forty years, twenty of them for entire summers, now an authentic old-timer, should feel, however anachronistically, one with my immigrant grandparents: except in the company of my new Jewish neighbors I always wonder how I am perceived and never feel as if I quite belong.

# HELP WANTED: OTHER WOMAN

MY 79-YEAR-OLD HUSBAND, the love of my life, is having an "affair" with a young single woman named Jenn. He and I fell in love more than a half century ago and have lived together for 22 years, but I have no regrets about the liaison. Go for it, I say. Be my guest.

In fact, it was Jenn herself, a self-described yogi with anarchist leanings, who told me about the affair after my husband confessed to feeling so guilty about it that he thought the time had come to tell the spouses.

I'm the one who hired her, and I could fire her, but I never will. I need her. When I checked out her references she was invariably described as a free spirit: centered, focused, patient, relaxed. One person said she was so unflappable that no matter what was happening around her she would sit perfectly still meditating for hours on end.

These are prime qualifications for my husband's companion, ever since he fell from a sleeping loft four years ago and suffered a traumatic brain injury. He was catapulted into a state resembling advanced Alzheimer's, left unable to remember anything that happened from then on or to find his way home from across the street. Caring for him requires, as people always tell me, the patience of a saint.

My husband is a gentleman and a sweetheart. Since his social skills, long-term memory and delight in life are pretty much intact, he is charming and considerate with people he knew before his fall.

But when a new companion arrives, for the first few weeks, until her face begins to look familiar, the constant presence of a stranger at his elbow can provoke in him such bouts of agitation, cursing (disinhibition) and combativeness that many a potential companion has quit on the second day.

"Today he threw a glass of water in my face," a recent hire told me in an e-mail message as she took her leave. "This is something I cannot accept, and I will not work with him."

In such situations I console myself by noting that the person who reacts with hurt or rage, despite having been told repeatedly that such attacks must never be taken personally, is not the right companion for my husband.

The drugs sometimes prescribed for these typical symptoms of frontal-lobe brain injury not only do nothing to soothe his agitation, but they also produce terrible side effects—in addition to which, according to recent studies, they work no better than placebos in the elderly.

As stated in the newspaper report on the largest study, and supported by most handbooks on caring for people with brain disease, the only reliable treatment for agitation like his is patience, calm and understanding.

When I asked Jenn at our interview if she thought she'd be able to withstand the shouting, cursing and threats of the early weeks, she said, "I can't think of much that can ruffle me."

The job of Scott's companion requires that she keep him happy and safe for hours every day, which means accompanying him to cafes, parks, the library, museums—all the places he went by himself before his fall—and never for an instant letting him out of her sight.

If only I could convince them of the dangers. If only they could know the panic I felt the time I lost him at the farmer's market in

Union Square and, after hours of combing the neighborhood in a police car, found him in the emergency room of St. Vincent's Hospital, agitated and in pain over three dislocated fingers. A stranger had found him lying on the cobblestones under the West Side Highway beside our empty shopping cart.

Or the time his companion lost him in the lobby of the Metropolitan Museum (which he referred to as his "temple" before his fall) after asking him to wait on a bench while she went to the bathroom, which of course he couldn't remember.

While the museum guards searched in his favorite galleries and I frantically notified the police, he, unaware that anything was amiss, had left the museum and, drawing on long-term memory, hailed a taxi to go home.

I assume he stiffed the driver because the emergency $20 bill I'd tucked inside his wallet hadn't been touched. Even though I'd been sick with worry, once he was safely home I felt proud of him for having found his way back on his own.

Most of his companions have been graduate students in the arts or the helping professions whom I found through postings on college Web sites. Jenn was the first person I hired through a popular Internet employment site.

Certain friends I consulted questioned how reliable a free-spirited yogi with anarchist leanings might be, especially one whose average stay on a job, according to her résumé, was under six months.

But she was signing on only for the summer, and I had a good feeling about her at the interview. I decided to give her a try.

My experience with new caregivers has left me so gun-shy that I wasn't prepared for the instant rapport Jenn established with Scott. How did she (or does she) do it?

Perhaps part of her appeal is that they look related: same ruddy skin that sunburns easily, same blondish hair (as his was before it turned white), same tall, slim, athletic build. To a stranger she might appear to be his granddaughter, and to him, she would seem a natural part of his intimate circle, one of the family.

But I believe her real secret is that she thinks the way he does. For instance, in the face of daunting Manhattan traffic, instead of reassuring him, as I and his other companions try to do (unsuccessfully), she—new to New York—shares his fears.

Walking beside him through the crowded streets, she seconds his disgust with smokers and horn blowers, his scorn for police and politicians, as readily as she joins in his passing delight at dachshunds, small children, architecture.

As far as I can tell, she sincerely agrees with the convictions he's held since his fall (and now freely expresses) that much of what goes on during an ordinary day is senseless or stupid. Instead of regarding his comments as incoherent rants, as others do, she sees in his dementia a kind of courage: a willingness to call the emperor naked.

Then perhaps it should not have surprised me that before the end of the second week, when other caregivers would barely be starting to earn his trust, she reported that he seemed to believe they were having an affair. She realized what was on his mind when he started speaking of his guilt about their "secret."

Not that he ever makes sexual advances or overtures toward her. She's assured me of that, and I believe her. He loves me more than ever, now that he's dependent. Besides, I'm sure that he, like me, has never been unfaithful, as we were in our earlier marriages.

It's just that without short-term memory to provide context, the events of daily life must seem incomprehensible or absurd, but being human, he can't stop trying to make sense of them anyway.

Imagination and ingenuity, those hallmarks of our species, are all it takes to explain anything, even a senseless world. From the moment Scott emerged from his drug-induced coma in the hospital, he started trying to explain his strange surroundings, alternately positing that he was in a sports club (seeing Tiger Woods on TV), a library (observing nurses with stacks of binders), a post office, a company headquarters, a hotel, even a French prison. (Noting that a passing male nurse in yellow scrubs looked uniformed, he shouted: "Look out! Here come the gendarmes with their gold braid!") Any place but a hospital, since, oblivious of his accident, he had no reason to imagine he was in an institution of healing.

Still unaware four years later that anything is wrong with him, how should he explain Jenn's constant presence? The one time I hired a male companion for him, he was certain that Henry was my lover. Why else would Henry hang around day after day?

Now that my husband's days are spent in the company of an attractive like-minded young woman who holds his hand wherever they go and acts like a soul mate, what better explanation can there be than that they're a couple? Even though he doesn't know, and will never know, her name. No contrary evidence or alternative account presents itself.

But if they are lovers, then he's betraying me, on whom he depends for everything—a predicament fraught with danger.

In his undamaged long-term memory he well recalls the strain that affairs put on his first marriage. When he asks me if I object to his spending so much time with "the people over there" (using a circumlocution characteristic of his disease), I rush to reassure him that not only do I not mind but, on the contrary, I benefit from it.

"Really?" he asks, incredulous, though visibly relieved. But as soon as something reminds him again of his predicament, I see him resume his struggle over whether or not to confess.

Soon, alas, the question will be moot. With summer's end, Jenn is getting ready to move on, leaving me to deal again with the agitation, foul language and perhaps violence with which Scott will likely test her replacement. Unless I am lucky enough to find another Jenn.

To that end, I have modified the "qualifications" section of my postings to include, "free-spirited, centered, focused, patient, relaxed," adding that "the calm that results from a strong yoga or meditation practice will be counted a definite plus."

The magic of attraction that makes a couple click remains ultimately inexplicable, as I am well aware. But like anyone who places a personals ad, I remain ever hopeful that love may strike again.

# CARING FOR AN ILL SPOUSE, AND FOR OTHER CAREGIVERS

MONDAY MORNING CAN BE a downer, but for the dozen women and men in our support group, it's a highlight of our week. That's when we gather to speak candidly of what is unspeakable in polite society or even among closest friends and family. We are the spouses or partners of people with dementia, an umbrella term for several degenerative, fatal brain diseases of which Alzheimer's is by far the most common. We are their primary caregivers; their lives depend on us.

Living with someone with dementia, who must be watched every minute, eventually becomes the central focus of a caregiver's life, as independence and freedom are replaced by stress and exhaustion. The members of our group, mostly in their eighties, are worn out by caring for their mates. Yet so lively are our Monday meetings that it sometimes takes two volunteer social workers to keep order: "Wait! Wait! One person at time!"

Often down or drained when we assemble, we part after 90 minutes buoyed and energized, week after week, year after year. (For me, four years and counting.) Not even a spouse's death keeps members away; a year after the funeral, our widows and widowers must be prodded to make way for those waiting to join.

According to the Alzheimer's Association, there are 15 million family members and friends providing unpaid care to people with dementia; hundreds of thousands of them meet regularly in support groups like ours to exchange information and understanding available nowhere else. Because science understands so little about dementia, we are the experts.

(To find a caregiver support group, contact the Alzheimer's Association, your local hospital or the Well Spouse Association, a nationwide group for people caring for spouses or partners.)

Our collective experience is a priceless resource. At a basic level, we exchange advice for keeping our partners from wandering off and techniques for bathing, calming and medicating them. We discuss ways to handle their hallucinations and incontinence, the mere mention of which often spooks outsiders. We share advice on what to tell the police, and what not to tell them, to keep them from hauling our sometimes violent mates to a psychiatric ward.

But our group's deepest value lies beyond such practical matters. We speak of feelings and problems too sensitive or fraught to discuss outside. We recount the disappearance of old friends, whose discomfort around our spouses keeps them away. We mourn the loss of companionship and sex. We guiltily admit to bouts of irrepressible anger in face of the intransigence and aggression typical of dementia. We speak about our children and stepchildren—some attentive and devoted, some interfering or remote.

And knowing that dementia is a terminal disease, together we contemplate death—our spouses' and our own. When should we refuse treatments or call in hospice? What will become of our loved ones if we die first? How will we manage our own final years as we rapidly exhaust our resources? These are deeply personal, in some ways political questions that science cannot answer.

One retired schoolteacher among us recalls that she was once too proud, shy and overwhelmed to consider joining a support group.

(Me too.) But after tentatively trying out our group in desperation, she stayed for a decade.

Her first reward was the group's urging that she find outside help to provide some relief. Then, over the years, the group was her sounding board when her husband became violent, emerged from a hospitalization unable to walk, lost his powers of speech, could no longer feed himself. As he approached the end, she asked the group to ponder with her whether to have a feeding tube inserted into his stomach.

After he died, she joined a bereavement group, then flew to Paris for a week. But when she returned, it was to our group—people who understood her and to whom she still had valuable knowledge to convey.

Since I joined it, our group has had an 80 percent turnover, mainly through death. Though our members have ranged from liberal to conservative and from financially secure to dependent on Medicaid, the distinctions that matter most are how long ago we received the dread diagnosis and what problems we are dealing with now.

With doctors unable to help us and Medicare reimbursement largely off limits, we turn to each other to learn what lies ahead as each of us descends the steps toward widowhood. Such grim knowledge occasionally causes a newcomer to bolt. But for those who remain, our support group is our lifeline.

When the last Congress unanimously endorsed a comprehensive plan to combat Alzheimer's disease, the lawmakers named improved caregiving as a major goal. If they are serious, they will vigorously promote support groups like ours and take advantage of our collective, hard-won experience.

# THE KENNING

IN HER BOOK *HIPPARCHIA'S CHOICE*, the French feminist philosopher Michelle Le Doueff develops a useful concept for assessing the relationship between how far we've come and how far we're going. She writes:

*Seventeenth-century English seafarers had a word to refer to the furthest visible point, corresponding to about twenty sea miles: the "kenning" . . . The kenning we need to give ourselves in politics is that of a generation: What should I be, do, demand, imagine today so that those who are now being born will from their earliest years discover an adult world in which some questions are settled, so they can see different ones? If we could establish today that all authorities or decision making bodies should be composed of equal numbers of men and women, sexism would very probably disappear from school textbooks. What a generation brought up in such a context could then think, what a truly mixed Parliament could concoct in the way of legislation are things that I cannot myself imagine because they go beyond my kenning.*

The horizon is a moving orbit. Already, because of feminism, many women today face prospects (for work, education, family) far freer than those my generation was born to, though in other ways (disparities between rich and poor, violence, environmental dangers, for example) things seem worse than ever. Knowing that young feminists already see a somewhat different world than I see (as my most vivid memories fade to history for them), I celebrate the very plasticity, or *movement*, that makes this possible—especially since one fact seems to light up the entire past twenty-five years: *There are no ex-feminists.* Ex-communists, ex-Republicans, ex-Catholics, ex-Moonies, ex-hippies, ex-convicts, ex-lovers. But as far as I know, no ex-feminists. Evidently, once that feminist light goes on it gleams so fiercely you sometimes almost wish you could turn it off and take a nap. But hardly anyone does. However frustrating the inevitable twenty-mile limit of our kenning, it *moves*, taking into its sweep new realms of consciousness to map and mold. That so much remains to be done means tremendous opportunity: just go out your door in the morning and something crucial will present itself.

As Rabbi Tarfon said centuries ago, "You are not required to complete the task, but neither are you free to abandon it."

Thus, feminism moves.

# SOURCES

MARRIAGE AND MEN

"A Marriage Agreement," *Up From Under*, August–September 1970; revised under the title "A Challenge to Every Marriage," *Redbook*, August 1971

"A Marriage Disagreement," *Dissent*, January 1998; *The Feminist Memoir Project*, ed. by Ann Snitow and Rachel DuPlessis, Crown, 1998

"Communication Between the Sexes: Breaking the Truce," talk given at Case Western Reserve University, winter 1983

SEX

"The War in the Back Seat," *Atlantic Monthly*, July 1972

"Organs and Orgasms," *Evergreen Review*, June 1971; Woman in Sexist Society, ed. by Vivian Gornick and B.K. Moran, Basic Books, 1971

"Sex and Power: Sexual Bases of Radical Feminism," *Signs*, Summer 1980 (vol. 5, no. 4)

WRITING

"The Taint," *Critical Fictions: the Politics of Imaginative Writing*, ed. by Philomena Mariani, Bay Press, 1991

"Women Writers in the Beat Generation," first published in somewhat different form under the title "The Beat Queens," *Village Voice Literary Supplement*, June 1989; revised and expanded under the title "Women Writers in the Beat Generation," *Kaimana*, 1993

"Living Our Life," *Between Women*, ed. by Carol Ascher, Louise DeSalvo, and Sarah Ruddick, Beacon Press, 1984

"Dances with Feminists," *Women's Review of Books*, January 1992

LATE LIFE

"Thoughts at Seventy," *Women's Review of Books*, July 2003

"Summer Jew," *Michigan Quarterly Review*, Winter 2003

"Help Wanted: Other Woman," *The New York Times*, Sept. 28, 2008

"Caring for an Ill Spouse, and Other Caregivers," *The New York Times*, May 10, 2011

"The Kenning," *Revisioning Feminism around the World*, Feminist Press, 1995

# EBOOKS BY ALIX KATES SHULMAN

## FROM OPEN ROAD MEDIA

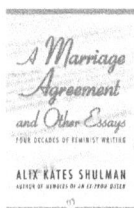

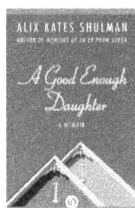

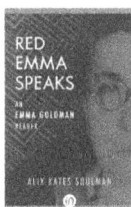

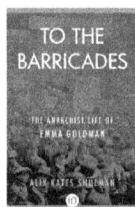

Available wherever ebooks are sold

OPEN ROAD

INTEGRATED MEDIA

OPEN (()) ROAD
INTEGRATED MEDIA

**Open Road Integrated Media** is a digital publisher and multimedia content company. Open Road creates connections between authors and their audiences by marketing its ebooks through a new proprietary online platform, which uses premium video content and social media.